ENGLAND

THE
OFFICIAL **ENGLAND**
WORLD CUP
GUIDE

ENGLAND

THE OFFICIAL ENGLAND WORLD CUP GUIDE

PaRragon

Bath · New York · Singapore · Hong Kong · Cologne · Delhi · Melbourne

First published by Parragon in 2010

Parragon
Queen Street House
4 Queen Street
Bath BA1 1HE, UK

TheFA.com

Produced by Parragon under licence by The Football Association Ltd.
All information correct at time of creation, December 2009
World rankings are official FIFA figures for November 2009.

ISBN 978-1-4075-9532-0

Printed in Spain

CONTENTS

INTRODUCTION

© PA Photos

England's name being shown by FIFA Secretary General Jerome Valcke as Charlize Theron looks on during the 2010 FIFA World Cup Draw.

At last the wait is almost over and all eyes are on South Africa as the 32 finalists assemble to take part in what for many is the world's most exciting sporting tournament.

It all began two or three years ago when over a hundred nations from six zones (Africa, Asia, Europe, North, Central America and Caribbean, Oceania and South America) were whittled down in qualifying matches that built to a climax in the November 2009 play-offs where a number of fancied teams faced inevitable disappointment. Notable European absentees include Russia, Croatia, Scotland and the Republic of Ireland.

THE FINAL DRAW

The draw for the Finals was staged in Cape Town on 4 December 2009 at the Cape Town International Convention Centre in a ceremony presented by the Oscar-winning South African actress Charlize Theron.

The seeding was based on the October 2009 FIFA ranking and seven squads joined hosts South Africa as seeded teams in Pot 1. Pot 2 was composed of teams from Asia, Oceania, and North and Central America and the Caribbean. Pot 3 included teams from Africa and South America. Pot 4 held the remaining European teams.

Geographical criteria meant that no two teams from the same confederation were drawn in the same group (except European teams, where a maximum of two could be in a group).

There are groups comprising three strong teams and one underdog, and there are groups where all four teams are evenly matched. But predicting anything is hard on this occasion, because nearly all the teams are going to encounter unfamiliar conditions such as playing at altitude and the South African winter. Johannesburg will play a key role in the World Cup, hosting the opening ceremony when a star-spangled cast of international celebrities from the worlds of show business, the music industry and politics will gather.

A GLOBAL GAME

It could be a World Cup full of surprises, with at least eight of the teams good enough to win it, plus a couple of strong unseeded teams like France and Portugal. At root the World Cup is an intercontinental duel between Western Europe and South America. The current score is nine cup wins per continental bloc and the strongest likelihood is that Brazil, Argentina, Germany, Italy, England and France (one World Cup each), Spain and the Netherlands (no wins) will make it through to the Quarter-finals. Any of these countries that haven't reached the fifth game of the tournament will be seen to have failed, while any other team breaking into that elite eight will legitimately claim a triumph.

In early June, when teams have settled into unfamiliar training compounds, coaches will make their final selections and gather their charges around them to select those they believe will lift the World Cup in just seven games' time.

The most sought after trophy of the most popular sport on the planet will, for the first time, be contested in an African country. From 11 June to 11 July, South Africa will host football's greatest spectacle and the beautiful game, a unifier of all peoples, will be witnessed by a global TV audience larger than the total population of Great Britain.

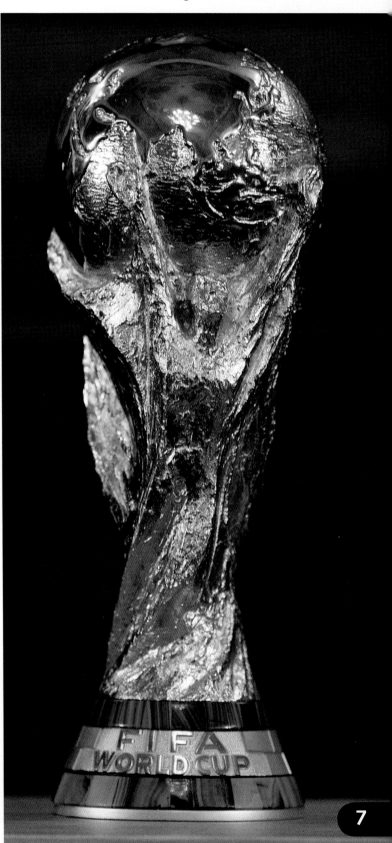

The famed 18-carat gold FIFA World Cup trophy which is presented to the winning team. The names of the winning countries are engraved on the underside of the base.

BOBBY MOORE

© PA Photos

FACT FILE

POSITION Defender
WORLD CUP CAPS 14
GOALS 0
WINS 8
DRAWS 2
LOSSES 4
WORLD CUP HONOURS
Winner 1966

Voted England's greatest ever footballer with over half the total votes, Bobby Moore earned 108 England caps, and captained a record 90 matches. Alongside these distinctions he also won the World Cup, the FA Cup, the European Cup Winners' Cup, and was Footballer of the Year in 1964.

Moore made his England debut in an international friendly 4-0 win against Peru in May 1962, and impressed then manager Walter Winterbottom so much he stayed in the team for the duration of the World Cup in Chile. By the time England crashed out to eventual tournament winners Brazil in the Quarter-finals, Moore was noted as one to watch.

The following year a 22-year-old Moore became the youngest ever England captain in what was only his 12th national appearance.

Already well established as England captain by the time Alf Ramsey took over as manager, Moore was central to the new tactical formation favoured by Ramsey – the 'wingless wonders'.

In the 1966 World Cup Final, England faced West Germany at Wembley Stadium and the stage was set for one of the greatest matches ever played. Tireless efforts and last-gasp goals meant that in extra-time, the score was 3-2 to England. While his team-mates were focused on lasting out the whistle, Moore calmly set up Geoff Hurst who made it 4-2 in the dying seconds of the game and Moore led the team to collect the trophy from Queen Elizabeth II.

Bobby Moore lifting the Jules Rimet trophy after England's glorious World Cup win in July 1966.

BOBBY CHARLTON

FACT FILE

POSITION Midfielder
WORLD CUP CAPS 14
GOALS 4
WINS 8
DRAWS 2
LOSSES 4
WORLD CUP HONOURS
Winner 1966

Legendary midfielder Bobby Charlton was the lynchpin of Alf Ramsey's 1966 World Cup-winning team as well as an inspirational role-model who survived the horror of the 1958 Munich air disaster which tragically claimed the lives of a number of team-mates from Manchester United.

A rare ability to play with either foot and a reputation for tireless energy during matches saw Charlton become a regular feature in England internationals during the 1960s, and he scored hat-tricks against the USA in 1959, and Mexico just two years later.

By the time he scored against Argentina in the 1962 World Cup Finals, Charlton had found the net 25 times in 38 appearances for England, and still holds the record for most goals scored at an impressive 49.

A skilful and powerful presence on the pitch, Charlton's reputation for long-range shots grew rapidly, and one such shot still holds a place as one of the most famous goals in Three Lions history. During the World Cup match against Mexico in 1966 he fired a shot into the top corner of the Mexico net from 25 yards away, typical modesty leading him to proclaim "I didn't really expect them to allow me to keep going... so I just banged it."

However, it was the two goals scored in the Semi-final against Portugal that cemented Charlton's international credentials, and although he failed to score during the Final against West Germany, there is no doubt that his persistence in attack was a major factor in the victory.

Bobby Charlton celebrates England's third goal during the World Cup Final between England and West Germany, 30.07.1966

© PA Photos

FACT FILE
POSITION Midfielder
WORLD CUP CAPS 8
GOALS 2
WINS 2
DRAWS 5
LOSSES 1
WORLD CUP HONOURS
Quarter-finals 1986, Semi-finals 1990

Bryan Robson, known affectionately as Captain Marvel, was the most complete midfielder of his day and one of the finest players to wear an England shirt in the 1980s and 1990s.

In 1982, the Manchester United man was an important part of Bobby Robson's England squad that qualified for the World Cup Finals for the first time since 1970.

In the first game against France, he scored one of the fastest goals in the history of the Finals when he found the back of the net in the very first minute of the game. He went on to score again in the second half and left the scoreboard a blistering 3-1 to England.

November 1982 saw Robson rewarded with the captaincy as he led England to a 3-0 defeat of Greece in Salonika. Throughout his career, Robson captained England 65 times, a total only exceeded by two others – Bobby Moore and Billy Wright.

Robson would almost certainly have reached the 100 cap mark for his country if it wasn't for injury, which caused him to miss crucial games in the 1986 and 1990 World Cups, including the 2-1 defeat against Argentina which sent England crashing out at the Quarter-finals of the 1986 World Cup.

International World Cup warm-up, Tunisia v England 02.06.1990

© PA Photos

FACT FILE

POSITION Striker
WORLD CUP CAPS 12
GOALS 10
WINS 5
DRAWS 4
LOSSES 3
WORLD CUP HONOURS
Quarter-finals 1986, Semi-finals 1990

Gary Lineker is one of the greatest forwards that English football has ever produced. He scored 48 international goals in 80 matches for his country, leaving him only one short of Sir Bobby Charlton's England record.

He entered the 1986 World Cup in Mexico after scoring 38 goals in 52 matches for Everton, and recovered from a series of early failures to score to a legendary hat-trick against Poland – which remains his own favourite goal-scoring memory. Lineker's scoring abilities made him the only English winner of the World Cup Golden Boot, a result of his six goals in the 1986 tournament in Mexico.

Lineker retained his form at the 1990 World Cup in Italy, making four vital strikes en route to the Semi-finals where despite a Lineker goal in the 80th minute which brought the score level, England lost to West Germany in an infamous and heartbreaking penalty shoot-out.

He played his last game for England against Sweden in Euro 92, eight years after he had made his international debut against Scotland.

Famously, Lineker was never sent off nor received a yellow card throughout a playing career that lasted an incredible 568 games. An achievement rewarded in 1990 with a FIFA Fair Play Award for England after the World Cup in Italy.

International Friendly
England v Hungary
12.09.1990

PELÉ

FACT FILE
POSITION Striker
WORLD CUP CAPS 13
GOALS 12
WINS 12
DRAWS 0
LOSSES 1
WORLD CUP HONOURS
Winner 1958, 1962, 1970

Pelé is generally accepted to be the greatest footballer ever. His grace, precision and killer instinct astounded his opponents and left the defeated unsure whether to applaud his skills or mourn their own loss.

The world was first introduced to the young Brazilian at the 1958 World Cup in Sweden when he took to the field and scored the single goal which defeated Wales in the Quarter-final. This goal made him the youngest World Cup scorer at 17 years and 239 days old.

In the Semi-final against France, Pelé once again shone with a second half hat-trick which sealed Brazil's 5-2 victory. Proving this was no fluke, he went on to rack up a further two goals in the Final to beat Sweden by another astonishing 5-2.

Injury kept him to a minimal role in the 1962 World Cup and he had to watch his team-mates once again lift the trophy before rejoining them and regaining the trophy for a third historic occasion in 1970.

After playing an incredible 1,366 competitive matches and scoring 1,283 first-class goals (12 in World Cup Finals), he became a footballing ambassador and, now approaching his 70th birthday, he will be there among the crowds for the 2010 World Cup in South Africa.

© PA Photo

DIEGO MARADONA

FACT FILE

POSITION Striker
WORLD CUP CAPS 21
GOALS 8
WINS 12
DRAWS 4
LOSSES 5
WORLD CUP HONOURS Winner 1986

The controversial figure of Diego Maradona made his first appearance for Argentina in April 1977 during a friendly. He made such an impact that coach Cesar Luis Menotti faced calls to include him in the squad for the 1978 World Cup on home soil. Menotti however felt he was too young.

By Spain 1982, Maradona was a regular at internationals and scored two of the four goals in a win against Hungary. Faced with superior marking from Italy and Brazil in the next round though, he couldn't break free to score and the cup holders went home empty handed.

Hungry to prove himself, Maradona set out to dominate at the next World Cup in Mexico 1986. He took the Golden Ball of the tournament and also scored two of the most famous, and infamous, goals in history.

In the Quarter-final against England, Maradona scored the 'Hand of God' goal, tipping the ball past 'keeper Peter Shilton. However, there can be no denying the skill behind his second goal, the FIFA Goal of the Century.

His run to score included 11 perfect touches. He dribbled past Glenn Hoddle, Peter Reid, Terry Fenwick and Terry Butcher before beating Shilton once more. Argentina beat England 2–1 and went on to defeat West Germany 3-2 in the Final. Now manager of Argentina, 2010 will be Maradona's first World Cup in charge.

© PA Photos

England's 14 matches with Argentina have included five in the World Cup, four Wembley friendlies and one in Buenos Aires that was abandoned when the pitch flooded.

Alf Ramsey's England faced the favourites Argentina in the Quarter-finals of the 1966 World Cup. From the first attack, it was clear that the South Americans were determined to beat England at all costs.

Visiting captain Antonio Rattin was sent off by the referee, and play was held up for seven minutes as Rattin demanded an interpreter before eventually leaving the field. Geoff Hurst headed the only goal from Peters' superb cross, and ill feeling was so strong by the end, that the traditional shirt-swapping didn't take place.

England's meeting with Argentina at the Mexico World Cup in 1986 was yet another electrifying match. The match sprang to life five minutes into the second period, Steve Hodge flicking a looping back-pass towards Peter Shilton. The subsequent clash saw Diego Maradona make his infamous 'Hand of God' goal, which the referee incredibly allowed to stand.

Four minutes later Maradona collected the ball just inside his own half and skipped past three hefty challenges before rifling home the goal of the tournament. Gary Lineker gave England hope with nine minutes left, but then missed when it seemed easier to score. England were out!

England again faced Argentina in the Second Round of the 1998 World Cup in France. Argentina scored with a penalty after five minutes, then England hit back to lead 2-1 with Alan Shearer's penalty and a wonderful Michael Owen goal that catapulted the 18-year-old to world stardom.

It was 2-2 at the break, and a bad-tempered kick on Diego Simeone saw David Beckham sent off, Sol Campbell had a goal disallowed, and England finally went out on penalties. There could hardly have been more drama.

World Cup Quarter-final match in Mexico. Argentina's Diego Maradona appears to handle the ball to score the opening goal. 22.06.1986

© PA Photos

England had to wait for their revenge at the next World Cup in the Far East. When the teams clashed in the second group fixture in Sapporo, Beckham's nerveless penalty after Pochettino's foul on Michael Owen in the 44th minute was enough to secure the points.

The two sides didn't meet at Germany 2006, both crashing out at the Quarter-finals, and although drawn in different groups, it's possible these old rivals will square up once more in South Africa. The stage is set.

David Beckham scores from the penalty mark during the 2002 World Cup, Group F match against Argentina at the Sapporo Dome, Japan 07.06.2002

ENGLAND 🏴󠁧󠁢󠁥󠁮󠁧󠁿 V

© PA Photos

England v West Germany, World Cup Final, Wembley Stadium, London. 30.07.1966

Gary Lineker, an England legend with 48 goals in 80 internationals, once said: "Football's a simple game. Twenty-two men chase after the ball and at the end the Germans win." Well, that's not strictly true. England beat West Germany nine times, twice when they were the reigning World Champions, and the unified Germany three times.

The English hosts had six consecutive victories against Germany under their belts when the two teams squared up that unforgettable July afternoon

at Wembley for the World Cup Final of 1966.

After a tentative first few minutes, Haller pounced to put West Germany in front. Six minutes later Bobby Moore, England's great captain, floated in a free-kick for West Ham team-mate Geoff Hurst to head the equaliser. Martin Peters' close-range goal 12 minutes from time looked to have won the World Cup for Alf Ramsey's England, but West Germany made it 2-2 in the dying seconds.

It was a match of almost unbearable tension and there was still more to come. Hurst's shot from Alan Ball's cross in extra-time hit the underside of the bar

GERMANY

and bounced down inches over the line, according to the Russian linesman. Moore, still calm and collected, lofted a long pass upfield for Hurst to blast home a fourth goal for England. He remains the only player to have scored a hat-trick in a World Cup Final.

Four years later the teams met again in a World Cup Quarter-final in Mexico. Things began to go wrong for England even before the match started – Gordon Banks, the brilliant goalkeeper was struck down with a stomach bug, and had to be replaced. England were still 2-0 up by the 49th minute and seemed to be coasting to victory, but the match ended in a shock 3-2 defeat.

There were more epic duels with West Germany in a World Cup Semi-final in 1990 and a European Championship Semi-final in 1996, both of which Germany won on penalties in extra-time.

But there was a night of pure joy for England fans as Germany were humbled 5-1 in Munich after a critical World Cup Qualifier in 2001. Michael Owen scored a hat-trick, the first by an England player against a German side since Geoff Hurst – and Steven Gerrard and Emile Heskey weighed in with the others.

Germany v England, European Qualifying Group 9
Olympic Stadium, Munich, 01.09.2001

SOUTH AFRICA:
11 JUNE 2010

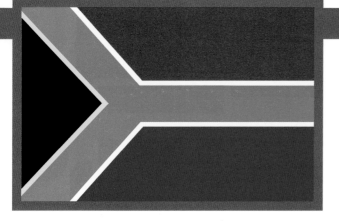

A huge building effort has resulted in five new stadiums and extensive improvements to existing stadiums in preparation for the 64 matches of the 2010 World Cup. Many stadiums will be officially relabelled during the tournament – the FIFA-approved names are used throughout.

CAPE TOWN (GREEN POINT)

This new stadium with a capacity of 70,000 is a stone's throw from the ocean and the mountains of Cape Town.

8 matches, including a Semi-final

DURBAN

The new stadium, holding 70,000, includes two large archways which will span the roof.

7 matches, including a Semi-final

JOHANNESBURG (ELLIS PARK)

Ellis Park was first built in 1928, rebuilt in 1982 and has now undergone a further upgrade. The stadium with a 61,000 capacity has also been used for the Rugby World Cup.

7 matches, including a Quarter-final

JOHANNESBURG (SOCCER CITY)

Soccer City is now the home of football in South Africa. The stadium with a 94,700 capacity has a unique design, with the outer part resembling an African pot.

8 matches, including the Final

MANGAUNG/BLOEMFONTEIN (FREE STATE)

This stadium in Mangaung/Bloemfontein has hosted matches in the CAF Africa Cup of Nations and the Rugby World Cup. A costly upgrade will increase the capacity to 48,000.

6 matches, including one in the Round of 16

NELSON MANDELA BAY/ PORT ELIZABETH

A new stadium holding 48,000 is being built on the North End Lake, making it an idyllic setting for match days. The three-tier design includes two rings of skyboxes.

8 matches, including the match for Third Place

TSHWANE/PRETORIA (LOFTUS VERSFELD)

In the heart of Tshwane/Pretoria, Loftus will be upgraded to bring it to a 50,000 capacity. The site has hosted matches in the CAF Africa Cup of Nations and is now home to Mamelodi Sundowns.

6 matches, including one in the Round of 16

NELSPRUIT (MBOMBELA)

The new stadium with its rounded rectangular shape and 46,000 capacity is close to game parks, allowing fans to see wildlife on rest days.

4 matches

POLOKWANE (PETER MOKABA)

Polokwane's new stadium will be situated in the Peter Mokaba Sports Complex, named after a political activist during apartheid. With its 46,000 capacity it will be a suitable addition to the Limpopo Province, where they have the country's largest number of registered footballers.

4 matches

© Getty Images, Inc.

RUSTENBURG (ROYAL BAFOKENG)

The Royal Bafokeng Sports Palace has a 42,000 capacity and has hosted many Premier League matches.

6 matches, including one in the Round of 16

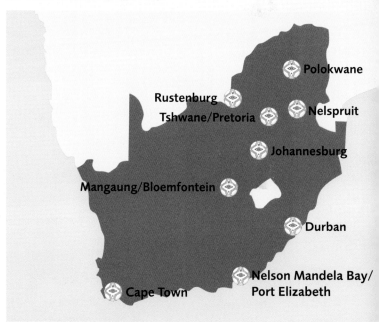

Right: Map of South Africa showing match venues
Below: Soccer City, Johannesburg

SOUTH AFRICA

Exuberant crowds will create a uniquely African atmosphere throughout this World Cup. Throughout the decades of apartheid, the fiercely competitive national league developed a level of proficiency and in 1992 'Bafana Bafana' ('The Boys') marked its post-apartheid international debut with a 1–0 victory over Cameroon. Four years later, South Africa lifted the African Nations Cup and then qualified for the World Cups in France 1998 and in Korea and Japan 2002.

All this amounted to South Africa being chosen as the first African country to host the World Cup. The 2009 Confederations Cup was a rehearsal for 2010, with South Africa hosting a competition featuring the champions of the world's six regional football federations, plus Italy as the current World Cup holder. South Africa reached the Semi-finals and came a credible fourth after losing 3–2 in the runners-up game against a weakened Spanish team. A brace of Katlego Mphela goals took the game to extra-time and provided a climax to the campaign.

South Africa v Spain, Confederations Cup,
Third Place Play-Off, Rustenburg 28.06.2009

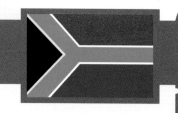

ROUTE TO THE FINALS

INTERNATIONAL MATCHES PLAYED IN THE RUN-UP TO THE WORLD CUP DRAW

14.06.09*	South Africa	0	0	Iraq
17.06.09*	South Africa	2	0	New Zealand
20.06.09*	South Africa	0	2	Spain
25.06.09*	South Africa	0	1	Brazil
28.06.09*	South Africa	2	3	Spain
12.08.09	South Africa	1	3	Serbia
05.09.09	Germany	2	0	South Africa
08.09.09	Republic of Ireland	1	0	South Africa
19.09.09	South Africa	1	0	Madagascar
10.10.09	Norway	1	0	South Africa
13.10.09	Iceland	1	0	South Africa
14.11.09	South Africa	0	0	Japan
17.11.09	South Africa	0	0	Jamaica

* FIFA Confederations Cup

FINALS GROUP A

SOUTH AFRICA

SOUTH AFRICA PLAY	COUNTRY	DATE	VENUE
	MEXICO	11.06.10	JOHANNESBURG - JSC
	URUGUAY	16.06.10	TSHWANE/PRETORIA
	FRANCE	22.06.10	MANGAUNG / BLOEMFONTEIN

VITAL STATISTICS

WORLD RANKING 86th
KEEPER AND DEFENCE 6/10
MIDFIELD 7/10
ATTACK 5/10

Mexico v El Salvador, World Cup Qualifier, Azteca Stadium, Mexico City, 10.10.2009

Mexico are now facing their fifth World Cup Finals in a row. In Germany 2006, they were one of eight top-seeded teams and progressed to a second-round defeat against Argentina.

Javier Aguirre, the former Mexican player and manager, turned things around with a run of five Qualifier wins, including one against the USA, their main local rivals. A second victory over the USA in the CONCACAF Gold Cup has convinced the Aztecas' fans that their troubles are behind them.

Players who stand out are two formidable defenders, the captain Rafael Márquez of Barcelona and the solid and aggressive left-back, Carlos Salcido of PSV Eindhoven. Others who could make a mark in South Africa are the midfielder Andrés Guardado and the goalkeeper Guillermo Ochoa. A forward to note is Arsenal's Carlos Vela, a 21-year-old who has shown promise for club and country. At the other end of the age range is Cuauhtémoc Blanco who has a fitness and brilliance that belies his years. He will be 37 in July 2010, but he put up a good case for his selection in the winning run that secured qualification.

ROUTE TO THE FINALS

CONCACAF FINAL STAGE – FINAL TABLE

TEAM	P	W	D	L	F	A	PTS
USA	10	6	2	2	19	13	20
MEXICO	10	6	1	3	18	12	19
HONDURAS	10	5	1	4	17	11	16
COSTA RICA	10	5	1	4	15	15	16
EL SALVADOR	10	2	2	6	9	15	8
TRINIDAD & TOBAGO	10	1	3	6	10	22	6

FINALS GROUP A

MEXICO PLAY		COUNTRY	DATE	VENUE
		SOUTH AFRICA	11.06.10	JOHANNESBURG - JSC
		FRANCE	17.06.10	POLOKWANE
		URUGUAY	22.06.10	RUSTENBURG

VITAL STATISTICS

WORLD RANKING 15th
KEEPER AND DEFENCE 7/10
MIDFIELD 6/10
ATTACK 5/10

URUGUAY

Uruguay won – as host nation – the inaugural World Cup in 1930, won again in 1950 in Brazil, and have qualified for a further eight World Cups. They are also the smallest nation to have lifted the World Cup.

However, Uruguay's World Cup record during the 21st century doesn't thrill. They tumbled out of the first round in 2002 and failed to qualify for 2006 after losing a play-off with Australia. For 2010 they struggled in their South American group and nearly came unstuck in a play-off against Costa Rica.

The man who catches the most criticism is manager Oscar Tabárez, who is in his second spell in charge having coached the team that qualified for Italy 1990. Tabárez has used the experience of thirty-something attackers Sebastián Abreu and Diego Forlán while bringing on new players such as goalkeeper Fernando Muslera, defender Diego Godín, midfielder Nicolás Lodeiro and striker Luis Suárez. All are ones to watch.

Over the years Uruguay have produced a huge number of world-class players – Diego Forlán, Álvaro Recoba, José Nasazzi, Obdulio Varela, Rodolfo Rodríguez – but the current question is whether Tabárez's blend of youth and experience can once again prove small is beautiful.

Uruguay v Costa Rica, World Cup play-off, Centenario Stadium, Montevideo, 18.11.2009

ROUTE TO THE FINALS

SOUTH AMERICA QUALIFYING GROUP – FINAL TABLE

TEAM	P	W	D	L	F	A	PTS
BRAZIL	18	9	7	2	33	11	34
CHILE	18	10	3	5	32	22	33
PARAGUAY	18	10	3	5	24	16	33
ARGENTINA	18	8	4	6	23	20	28
URUGUAY	18	6	6	6	28	20	24
ECUADOR	18	6	5	7	22	26	23
COLOMBIA	18	6	5	7	14	18	23
VENEZUELA	18	6	4	8	23	29	22
BOLIVIA	18	4	3	11	22	36	15
PERU	18	3	4	11	11	34	13

SOUTH AMERICA/OCEANIA PLAY-OFF

COSTA RICA	0	1	URUGUAY
URUGUAY	1	1	COSTA RICA

FINALS GROUP A

URUGUAY

URUGUAY PLAY	COUNTRY	DATE	VENUE
	FRANCE	11.06.10	CAPE TOWN
	SOUTH AFRICA	16.06.10	TSHWANE/PRETORIA
	MEXICO	22.06.10	RUSTENBURG

VITAL STATISTICS

WORLD RANKING 19th
KEEPER AND DEFENCE 5/10
MIDFIELD 5/10
ATTACK 6/10

France v Republic of Ireland, World Cup Qualifier, play-off second leg, Stade de France, Paris, 18.11.2009

Thierry Henry's handball in the dying seconds of the World Cup play-off against the Republic of Ireland will haunt this team. They must follow the magnificent group of players who united France in style and grace when they won the World Cup in 1998 and then the European Championship two years later. The legacy seemed permanent and at the 2006 World Cup Final it took the combination of a Zinédine Zidane dismissal, and a penalty shoot-out with Italy to defeat them. Further back, France were World Cup Semi-finalists in 1958, 1982 and 1986. Along the way, they have been Brazil's most formidable World Cup Finals opponents, having won two, drawn one and lost one in four high-level encounters.

Recent glories have eluded them, however – a sterile Euro 2008 campaign disappointed, and poor form continued into World Cup qualification with a stuttering second place in an easy group. However, their qualification struggle may well be an unreliable guide to how they will play in South Africa. Assuming that Thierry Henry, Nicolas Anelka and Franck Ribéry are on form – then France have great potential. In addition, Bacary Sagna, Éric Abidal, William Gallas and Patrice Evra could be an awesome foursome if they gel into the kind of defensive unit they operate in at club level.

ROUTE TO THE FINALS

EUROPE QUALIFYING GROUP 7 – FINAL TABLE

TEAM	P	W	D	L	F	A	PTS
SERBIA	10	7	1	2	22	8	22
FRANCE	10	6	3	1	18	9	21
AUSTRIA	10	4	2	4	14	15	14
LITHUANIA	10	4	0	6	10	11	12
ROMANIA	10	3	3	4	12	18	12
FAROE ISLANDS	10	1	1	8	5	20	4

EUROPE PLAY-OFFS

REPUBLIC OF IRELAND	0	1	FRANCE
FRANCE	1	1	REPUBLIC OF IRELAND

FINALS GROUP A
FRANCE

FRANCE PLAY	COUNTRY	DATE	VENUE
	URUGUAY	11.06.10	CAPE TOWN
	MEXICO	17.06.10	POLOKWANE
	SOUTH AFRICA	22.06.10	MANGAUNG / BLOEMFONTEIN

VITAL STATISTICS

WORLD RANKING 7th
KEEPER AND DEFENCE 8/10
MIDFIELD 7/10
ATTACK 9/10

ARGENTINA

Argentina's struggle to qualify for the 2010 World Cup gives pause for thought, but certainly doesn't rule them out. Brazil struggled to qualify in 2002, and then won the cup while Argentina sailed through qualification only to fall at the group stage.

La Selección's four World Cup Final appearances and two wins plus a record 14 Copa América titles is a set of impressive winning statistics. The current squad is also strong, with a host of players who would make it onto any team-sheet in the world. However, even with such players on call, there was a 6–1 thrashing by Bolivia in April 2009 and shortly after a string of three defeats, before two late goals in the last two games clinched qualification.

There has been a reliance on older players, particularly Juan Sebastián Verón. In a warm-up game immediately prior to the Qualifier that Argentina lost 3–1 to Brazil, Rolando Schiavi made his international debut – he was 36. A 35-year-old striker, Martin Palermo, had languished until he was called up for the penultimate Qualifier against Peru. In Palermo's previous international – in 1999 – he had missed three penalties in one match against Colombia in the Copa América. But time as well as logic were defied when Palermo kept Argentina's World Cup aspirations alive with the winning goal against Peru in the third minute of added time.

Under Diego Maradona's management the stage is set for some memorable football, and a possible meeting between England and Argentina will create additional excitement.

Argentina v Peru, World Cup Qualifier,
Monumental Stadium, Buenos Aires, 10.10.2009

ROUTE TO THE FINALS

SOUTH AMERICA QUALIFYING GROUP – FINAL TABLE

TEAM	P	W	D	L	F	A	PTS
BRAZIL	18	9	7	2	33	11	34
CHILE	18	10	3	5	32	22	33
PARAGUAY	18	10	3	5	24	16	33
ARGENTINA	18	8	4	6	23	20	28
URUGUAY	18	6	6	6	28	20	24
ECUADOR	18	6	5	7	22	26	23
COLOMBIA	18	6	5	7	14	18	23
VENEZUELA	18	6	4	8	23	29	22
BOLIVIA	18	4	3	11	22	36	15
PERU	18	3	4	11	11	34	13

FINALS GROUP B

ARGENTINA

ARGENTINA PLAY	COUNTRY	DATE	VENUE
	NIGERIA	12.06.10	JOHANNESBURG - JEP
	KOREA REPUBLIC	17.06.10	JOHANNESBURG - JEP
	GREECE	22.06.10	POLOKWANE

VITAL STATISTICS
WORLD RANKING 8th
KEEPER AND DEFENCE 7/10
MIDFIELD 7/10
ATTACK 8/10

29

NIGERIA

© Getty Images, Inc.

Nigeria v Kenya, World Cup Qualifier,
Nairobi, 14.11.2009

On paper, Nigeria appear to be the best team in Africa, better surely than Ghana or South Africa and with the edge on arch-rivals Cameroon and the more fancied Côte d'Ivoire. Yet Nigeria haven't lifted a trophy since winning the African Nations Cup in 1994. They made World Cup appearances in 1994 and 1998, coming close to reaching the Quarter-finals, but in 2002 they were outgunned in a group that contained England, Sweden and Argentina, and failed to qualify for the 2006 World Cup.

Nigeria took it to the wire for 2010 qualification. The player they must thank for that is Mozambique's Dário, whose shock goal against Tunisia on 11 November 2009 allowed Nigeria to sneak past the Tunisians and through to qualification with a 3–2 away win in Kenya. Nigeria's scorers in that emotional victory were Obafemi Martins and Yakubu Aiyegbeni.

It now remains for manager Shaibu Amodu to improve on the organisation of players in order to exploit properly the defensive brilliance of Joseph Yobo; the classy midfield work of Mikel; the attacking flair of Obafemi Martins and the laid-back trickery of Kanu.

ROUTE TO THE FINALS

AFRICA QUALIFYING GROUP B – FINAL TABLE

TEAM	P	W	D	L	F	A	PTS
NIGERIA	6	3	3	0	9	4	12
TUNISIA	6	3	2	1	7	4	11
MOZAMBIQUE	6	2	1	3	3	5	7
KENYA	6	1	0	5	5	11	3

FINALS GROUP B

NIGERIA

NIGERIA PLAY	COUNTRY	DATE	VENUE
	ARGENTINA	12.06.10	JOHANNESBURG - JEP
	GREECE	17.06.10	MANGAUNG / BLOEMFONTEIN
	KOREA REPUBLIC	22.06.10	DURBAN

VITAL STATISTICS

WORLD RANKING 22nd
KEEPER AND DEFENCE 6/10
MIDFIELD 7/10
ATTACK 6/10

KOREA REPUBLIC

Korea Republic are now poised for a seventh successive World Cup appearance and fervently hoping to exceed the achievements of eight years ago.

As co-hosts with Japan of the 2002 World Cup, Korea Republic's greatest footballing hour came under Guus Hiddink. He led the Taeguk Warriors to victories against Italy and Spain on the way to a glorious 1–0 Semi-final defeat against Germany. In Germany 2006 the team fell at the group stages, but the latest World Cup campaign saw a change of tack with the 2007 managerial appointment of a Korean manager, Huh Jung-Moo.

Huh exploits the experience of players who are familiar with European club football and then blends that know-how with more youthful home-nurtured

talent. He led his team through a patchy, if unbeaten, qualifying run that began with a 4–0 home victory against Turkmenistan. High hopes were replaced by anxiety following draws to Korea DPR in Shanghai and then at home against Jordan. Three victories followed including the 1–0 defeat of arch-rivals Korea DPR that saw the two Korean nations finish jointly at the top of the table.

Korea Republic will be a team to beat, especially if star players fulfil expectations in high energy, high pressure counter-attacking line-ups. Look out for Park Ji-Sung, who has announced this will be his last World Cup. Park Chu-Young is another one to watch, a player in his prime who can score from both free kicks and open play.

Korea Republic v Korea DPR, World Cup Qualifier, World Cup Stadium, Seoul, 01.04.09

ROUTE TO THE FINALS

ASIA QUALIFYING FINAL GROUP 2 – FINAL TABLE

TEAM	P	W	D	L	F	A	PTS
KOREA REPUBLIC	8	4	4	0	12	4	16
KOREA DPR	8	3	3	2	7	5	12
SAUDI ARABIA	8	3	3	2	8	8	12
IRAN	8	2	5	1	8	7	11
UNITED ARAB EMIRATES	8	0	1	7	6	17	1

FINALS GROUP B

KOREA REPUBLIC

KOREA REPUBLIC PLAY	COUNTRY	DATE	VENUE
	GREECE	12.06.10	NELSON MANDELA BAY/PORT ELIZABETH
	ARGENTINA	17.06.10	JOHANNESBURG - JSC
	NIGERIA	22.06.10	DURBAN

VITAL STATISTICS

WORLD RANKING 52nd
KEEPER AND DEFENCE 6/10
MIDFIELD 6/10
ATTACK 6/10

GREECE

© Getty Images, Inc.

Greece v Ukraine, World Cup Qualifier play-off, first leg, Olympic Stadium, Athens, 14.11.2009

When Greece met Portugal in the 2004 European Championship Final, they emerged as 1–0 winners and 'King Otto' of Greece assumed his place at the centre of Greek culture.

Otto Rehhagel is still in charge and has engineered his adoptive country their second World Cup appearance having had the good fortune to find themselves in a lightweight qualifying group.

Rehhagel is credited with honing the leadership skills of the captain, Giorgos Karagounis. The Panathinaikos midfielder is seen as a fit replacement for Thodoris Zagorakis who led the team to victory at Euro 2004. Goalkeeper Alexandros Tzorvas put in some outstanding performances during qualification, while attackers to watch for are Dimitris Salpigidis of Panathinaikos and Celtic's Georgios Samaras. Theofanis Gekas of Bayer Leverkusen was the top-scoring European with 10 goals in the run-up to World Cup qualification.

ROUTE TO THE FINALS

EUROPE QUALIFYING GROUP 2 – FINAL TABLE

TEAM	P	W	D	L	F	A	PTS
SWITZERLAND	10	6	3	1	18	8	21
GREECE	10	6	2	2	20	10	20
LATVIA	10	5	2	3	18	15	17
ISRAEL	10	4	4	2	20	10	16
LUXEMBOURG	10	1	2	7	4	25	5
MOLDOVA	10	0	3	7	6	18	3

EUROPE PLAY-OFFS

GREECE	0	0	UKRAINE
UKRAINE	0	1	GREECE

FINALS GROUP B

GREECE PLAY	COUNTRY	DATE	VENUE
	KOREA REPUBLIC	12.06.10	NELSON MANDELA BAY/PORT ELIZABETH
	NIGERIA	17.06.10	MANGAUNG / BLOEMFONTEIN
	ARGENTINA	22.06.10	POLOKWANE

VITAL STATISTICS
WORLD RANKING 12th
KEEPER AND DEFENCE 6/10
MIDFIELD 5/10
ATTACK 5/10

ENGLAND

The Premiership is the world's most widely televised league and has nurtured a generation of talented and big match-hardened players. Combined with a favourable first-round draw, England find themselves in a relatively easy group and with a real chance for victory in South Africa. Throughout a powerful qualifying campaign, the arguments surrounding English World Cup optimism have filled the press and the airwaves.

England won the World Cup in 1966 and has maintained a consistent position as a top ten world side with a presence at every tournament since 1994. Fabio Capello is an experienced, unshakeable manager who carefully selects players from the best league in the world. The key players have immense experience and are playing at the top of their game. England's time has come, although the prospect of a penalty shoot-out is still cause for concern.

© Getty Images, Inc.

England v Croatia, World Cup Qualifier,
Wembley Stadium, London, 09.09.2009

ENGLAND v CROATIA
9 September 2009 WEMBLEY STADIUM

Nationwide
THE ENGLAND TEAM SPONSOR

ROUTE TO THE FINALS

EUROPE QUALIFYING FINAL GROUP 6 – FINAL TABLE

TEAM	P	W	D	L	F	A	PTS
ENGLAND	10	9	0	1	34	6	27
UKRAINE	10	6	3	1	21	6	21
CROATIA	10	6	2	2	19	13	20
BELARUS	10	4	1	5	19	14	13
KAZAKHSTAN	10	2	0	8	11	29	6
ANDORRA	10	0	0	10	3	39	0

FINALS GROUP C

ENGLAND

ENGLAND PLAY	COUNTRY	DATE	VENUE
	USA	12.06.10	RUSTENBURG
	ALGERIA	18.06.10	CAPE TOWN
	SLOVENIA	23.06.10	NELSON MANDELA BAY/PORT ELIZABETH

VITAL STATISTICS

WORLD RANKING 9th
KEEPER AND DEFENCE 8/10
MIDFIELD 8/10
ATTACK 8/10

USA

© Getty Images, Inc.

*USA v Brazil, Confederations Cup Final,
Ellis Park Stadium, Johannesburg, 28.06.2009*

America's national side approaches a sixth successive World Cup Finals ranked 14th in the world. That ranking reflects their form in the 2009 Confederations Cup, a campaign that included a 2–0 Semi-final victory over Spain, that ended Spain's 35-game unbeaten run and a 15-game winning streak. There was no shame in losing the Final 2–3 to a full-strength Brazil, particularly after leading 2–0 at half-time. In fact, the United States have often proved that big reputations are there to be punctured. Their 1–0 victory against England in the 1950 World Cup was one of football's greatest upsets, and they reached the Quarter-finals of the 2002 World Cup. However, American optimism was punctured in the 2006 World Cup when they were drawn in the 'group of death'.

Manager Bob Bradley has drawn on the country's youth system to prepare a squad combining overseas players with up-and-comers from Major League Soccer.

Much will depend on Clint Dempsey, who hit form in the Confederations Cup, scoring three goals. Dempsey was awarded the Bronze Ball for the tournament's third best individual performance.

ROUTE TO THE FINALS

CONCACAF FINAL STAGE – FINAL TABLE

TEAM	P	W	D	L	F	A	PTS
USA	10	6	2	2	19	13	20
MEXICO	10	6	1	3	18	12	19
HONDURAS	10	5	1	4	17	11	16
COSTA RICA	10	5	1	4	15	15	16
EL SALVADOR	10	2	2	6	9	15	8
TRINIDAD & TOBAGO	10	1	3	6	10	22	6

FINALS GROUP C

USA PLAY

	COUNTRY	DATE	VENUE
	ENGLAND	12.06.10	RUSTENBURG
	SLOVENIA	18.06.10	JOHANNESBURG - JEP
	ALGERIA	23.06.10	TSHWANE/ PRETORIA

VITAL STATISTICS

WORLD RANKING 14th
KEEPER AND DEFENCE 6/10
MIDFIELD 6/10
ATTACK 6/10

ALGERIA

Known as Les Fennecs, Algeria were once the hope of African football. In the 1982 World Cup they recorded a famous 2–1 victory over West Germany, eventual finalists. They were back in World Cup action in 1986, and won the African Nations Cup in 1990, but then they faded. Algerian qualification for 2010 couldn't have been more tense, on and off the field. Their qualifying matches against arch-rivals Egypt spawned riots that spread from North Africa to France. The necessity for a play-off was the result of a statistical freak that left both teams level in their group on points (13), goal difference (5) and goals scored (9). The play-off was in neutral Sudan and required 15,000 police to keep the peace among 30,000 spectators.

Since recognition in 1962, Algeria have gone through 34 managers, and current success may be due to the relative stability of having had Rabah Saâdane in charge for the past three years. Saâdane, a former Algeria defender, has moulded a team that is more European than African in style. Cautious 4-4-2 formations put defence at a premium and anything exciting is likely to flow through the versatile midfielder Karim Ziani.

Algeria v Egypt, World Cup Qualifier,
Cairo International Stadium, Cairo, 14.11.2009

ROUTE TO THE FINALS

AFRICA QUALIFYING GROUP C – FINAL TABLE

TEAM	P	W	D	L	F	A	PTS
ALGERIA	7	5	1	1	10	4	16
EGYPT	7	4	1	2	9	5	13
ZAMBIA	6	1	2	3	2	5	5
RWANDA	6	0	2	4	1	8	2

AFRICA PLAY-OFFS

ALGERIA	1	0	EGYPT

FINALS GROUP C

ALGERIA

ALGERIA PLAY	COUNTRY	DATE	VENUE
	SLOVENIA	13.06.10	POLOKWANE
	ENGLAND	18.06.10	CAPE TOWN
	USA	23.06.10	TSHWANE/ PRETORIA

VITAL STATISTICS

WORLD RANKING 28th
KEEPER AND DEFENCE 6/10
MIDFIELD 5/10
ATTACK 5/10

SLOVENIA

Slovenia conceded only four goals in qualifying from a group that included Poland, the Czech Republic and Slovakia.

Slovenia's opponents in South Africa should be warned that any teams that take Slovenia on must plan to staunch the flow of passes from Dedič and to keep the Köln forward Milivoje Novakovič under control. He scored five goals in qualifying.

Slovenia's form since the team was created after the break-up of Yugoslavia in 1991 is of qualified success. They got to the 2002 World Cup without losing a match, recording six wins and six draws. However, they lost all three games at the Finals. Two years later they were at Euro 2004 and now they have once again fought through to a big stage. Italy will treat Slovenia with respect having lost to them 0–1 in a 2006 World Cup Qualifier. And England players will recall that it took a penalty to secure England's 2–1 win against them in a September 2009 friendly. This is not a side to be taken lightly.

Slovenia v San Marino, World Cup Qualifier,
Stadio Olympico, Serravalle, 14.10.2009

ROUTE TO THE FINALS

EUROPE QUALIFYING GROUP 3 – FINAL TABLE

TEAM	P	W	D	L	F	A	PTS
SLOVAKIA	10	7	1	2	22	10	22
SLOVENIA	10	6	2	2	18	4	20
CZECH REPUBLIC	10	4	4	2	17	6	16
NORTHERN IRELAND	10	4	3	3	13	9	15
POLAND	10	3	2	5	19	14	11
SAN MARINO	10	0	0	10	1	47	0

EUROPE PLAY-OFFS

RUSSIA	2	1	SLOVENIA
SLOVENIA	1	0	RUSSIA

FINALS GROUP C

SLOVENIA

SLOVENIA PLAY	COUNTRY	DATE	VENUE
	ALGERIA	13.06.10	POLOKWANE
	USA	18.06.10	JOHANNESBURG - JEP
	ENGLAND	23.06.10	NELSON MANDELA BAY/PORT ELIZABETH

VITAL STATISTICS

WORLD RANKING 33rd
KEEPER AND DEFENCE 6/10
MIDFIELD 6/10
ATTACK 5/10

43

GERMANY

© Getty Images, Inc.

Germany v Finland, World Cup Qualifier,
HSH Nordbank Arena, Hamburg, 14.10.2009

Germany made heavy work of winning a featherweight World Cup qualifying group. But German national sides have a long record of being more than the sum of their parts.

Germany have won the World Cup three times, behind Brazil (five titles) and Italy (four titles), and have finished as runners-up four times, two more than any other side. There have been 11 Semi-final showings and at least a Quarter-final finish for the past 14 World Cups although their last World Cup Final victory was in 1990.

Two successive managers have built a team around the attack-minded midfield guile of Michael Ballack, the stand-out superstar of the team. And now, the previously inconsistent management which saw three different coaches in six years, seems to be behind them, this could be the year German football is reborn.

ROUTE TO THE FINALS

EUROPE QUALIFYING GROUP 4 – FINAL TABLE

TEAM	P	W	D	L	F	A	PTS
GERMANY	10	8	2	0	26	5	26
RUSSIA	10	7	1	2	19	6	22
FINLAND	10	5	3	2	14	14	18
WALES	10	4	0	6	9	12	12
AZERBAIJAN	10	1	2	7	4	14	5
LIECHTENSTEIN	10	0	2	8	2	23	2

FINALS GROUP D

GERMANY PLAY	COUNTRY	DATE	VENUE
	AUSTRALIA	13.06.10	DURBAN
	SERBIA	18.06.10	NELSON MANDELA BAY/PORT ELIZABETH
	GHANA	23.06.10	JOHANNESBURG - JSC

VITAL STATISTICS

WORLD RANKING 6th
KEEPER AND DEFENCE 6/10
MIDFIELD 7/10
ATTACK 7/10

AUSTRALIA

Australia have emerged as a 21st-century footballing force with the Socceroos poised to travel across the Southern hemisphere for a second successive World Cup appearance.

For 2010 Australia is looking to go beyond the 2006 second-round milestone when the unfancied side finally succumbed to an injury-time penalty awarded to Italy, the eventual champions.

There is a growing swagger in the disciplined way the Australian team has approached games in the run-up to South Africa. The ease of qualification has bolstered confidence, with Australia dominating its qualifying group. The team earned a maximum 10 points from the opening five matches to ensure progression to the final qualifying round with a game to spare. Add real playing determination and Australia could go far.

Australia v Japan, World Cup Qualifier,
Melbourne Cricket Ground, Melbourne, 17.06.2009

© Getty Images, Inc.

ROUTE TO THE FINALS

ASIA QUALIFYING FINAL GROUP 1 – FINAL TABLE

TEAM	P	W	D	L	F	A	PTS
AUSTRALIA	8	6	2	0	12	1	20
JAPAN	8	4	3	1	11	6	15
BAHRAIN	8	3	1	4	6	8	10
QATAR	8	1	3	4	5	14	6
UZBEKISTAN	8	1	1	6	5	10	4

FINALS GROUP D

AUSTRALIA PLAY	COUNTRY	DATE	VENUE
	GERMANY	13.06.10	DURBAN
	GHANA	19.06.10	RUSTENBURG
	SERBIA	23.06.10	NELSPRUIT

VITAL STATISTICS
WORLD RANKING 21st
KEEPER AND DEFENCE 6/10
MIDFIELD 6/10
ATTACK 5/10

SERBIA

© Getty Images, Inc.

Serbia v France, World Cup Qualifier,
Stadion Crvena Zvezda, Belgrade, 09.09.2009

Balkan politics meant that Serbians played for Yugoslavia until 2003, then for Serbia and Montenegro until the last World Cup, and now as Serbia. National excitement could not be running higher.

The manager, Radomir Antić came out of retirement to take over his national team in 2008. Older British fans will remember him as Raddy Antić, the Luton Town defender who, in 1983, scored the last-gasp winner against Manchester City, his famous goal simultaneously saving Luton from relegation and condemning City to the drop. Antić's managerial career provided even more drama and he is the only person to have managed all three Spanish giants Barcelona, Real Madrid, and Atlético Madrid.

Political redefinition has resulted in Antić losing several old hands from Montenegro in a squad that has fewer players from the 2006 campaign than any other country, and now has an entirely new attack. Serbia's two best known players are the captain Dejan Stanković of Inter Milan and Nemanja Vidić of Manchester United. On form, Stanković midfield versatility and shooting power make him a match winner. Vidić is the more reliable performer and his pacy positional sense qualifies him as one of the top defenders in the world.

ROUTE TO THE FINALS

EUROPE QUALIFYING GROUP 7 – FINAL TABLE

TEAM	P	W	D	L	F	A	PTS
SERBIA	10	7	1	2	22	8	22
FRANCE	10	6	3	1	18	9	21
AUSTRIA	10	4	2	4	14	15	14
LITHUANIA	10	4	0	6	10	11	12
ROMANIA	10	3	3	4	12	18	12
FAROE ISLANDS	10	1	1	8	5	20	4

FINALS GROUP D

SERBIA PLAY	COUNTRY	DATE	VENUE
	GHANA	13.06.10	TSHWANE/ PRETORIA
	GERMANY	18.06.10	NELSON MANDELA BAY/PORT ELIZABETH
	AUSTRALIA	23.06.10	NELSPRUIT

VITAL STATISTICS

WORLD RANKING 20th
KEEPER AND DEFENCE 7/10
MIDFIELD 6/10
ATTACK 5/10

GROUP D TEAM 3

GHANA

Ghana are star turns on their own continent having won the Africa Cup of Nations four times. This is their second successive appearance in the World Cup Finals.

In 2006, Ghana was the only African side to advance beyond the group stages, with famous victories over the Czech Republic and the USA. The nation went wild with anticipation but fate didn't favour them for their star player, Michael Essien, was suspended and the draw put them up against Brazil, who won 3–0.

The key players from the 2006 World Cup squad are still in place and will go to South Africa older, wiser and better practised at club level. The main striker

Matthew Amoah plays for Breda while defenders John Mensah and John Pantsil play for Sunderland and Fulham respectively. European club credentials are more impressive in midfield with the key duo of Michael Essien (Chelsea) and Sulley Muntari (Inter Milan) having it in their power to dictate the pace of any game.

Ghana has traditionally looked to Europe for managerial expertise and discipline to make the most of the available skills. In 2010 the man charged with melding this talent into an international unit is Milovan Rajevac. Hopes are high for the way he has guided the side into an efficient 4-4-2 line-up that has pushed forward fearlessly during qualifying games.

Ghana v Zambia, International friendly, Brisbane Road, London, 12.08.2009

ROUTE TO THE FINALS

AFRICA QUALIFYING GROUP D – FINAL TABLE

TEAM	P	W	D	L	F	A	PTS
GHANA	6	4	1	1	9	3	13
BENIN	6	3	1	2	6	6	10
MALI	6	2	3	1	8	7	9
SUDAN	6	0	1	5	2	9	1

FINALS GROUP D

GHANA PLAY	COUNTRY	DATE	VENUE
	SERBIA	13.06.10	TSHWANE/ PRETORIA
	AUSTRALIA	19.06.10	RUSTENBURG
	GERMANY	23.06.10	JOHANNESBURG - JSC

VITAL STATISTICS

WORLD RANKING 37th
KEEPER AND DEFENCE 6/10
MIDFIELD 7/10
ATTACK 5/10

© Getty Images, Inc.

Netherlands v England, International friendly,
Amsterdam Arena, Amsterdam, 12.08.2009

The Dutch have consistently featured as flair players and managers for top European clubs, making Holland the most talented national team never to have won the World Cup.

The Oranjes reached two Finals in the 1970s against West Germany and Argentina, but from the 1980s Dutch teams suffered ill-disciplined decades of World Cup underachievement including a failure to qualify in 2002. In 2006, the Netherlands lost 1–0 to Portugal in the second round 'Battle of Nuremberg', a match that produced a record 16 yellow and four red cards.

Bert van Marwijk, national team manager since 2008, is a straight-talking realist whose long career in football has largely been in the Netherlands. He led a talented group of players through a flawless winning run of qualifying games for the 2010 competition. With players like Dirk Kuyt, Nigel de Jong, Arjen Robben, Wesley Sneijder, Rafael van der Vaart and Robin van Persie at the peak of their game, Holland's chance are good.

ROUTE TO THE FINALS

EUROPE QUALIFYING FINAL GROUP 9 – FINAL TABLE

TEAM	P	W	D	L	F	A	PTS
NETHERLANDS	8	8	0	0	17	2	24
NORWAY	8	2	4	2	9	7	10
SCOTLAND	8	3	1	4	6	11	10
FYR MACEDONIA	8	2	1	5	5	11	7
ICELAND	8	1	2	5	7	13	5

FINALS GROUP E

NETHERLANDS PLAY	COUNTRY	DATE	VENUE
	DENMARK	14.06.10	JOHANNESBURG - JSC
	JAPAN	19.06.10	DURBAN
	CAMEROON	24.06.10	CAPE TOWN

VITAL STATISTICS

WORLD RANKING 3rd
KEEPER AND DEFENCE 8/10
MIDFIELD 7/10
ATTACK 7/10

DENMARK

Denmark won the 1992 European Championship Final and reached the World Cup Quarter-finals against Brazil in 1998 but then lost their way, failing to qualify for the last European or World Cups. That said, England fans might recall friendly matches that had the Danes beating England 4–1 in 2005, and 3–2 in 2003.

The roll-call of former Danish stars includes Allan Simonsen, brothers Michael and Brian Laudrup, Peter Schmeichel and Morten Olsen. Olsen, the team captain who played 102 games for Denmark between 1970 and 1989, has been Danish manager since 2000. He generally favours an attacking style, exploiting the midfield passing skills of Christian Poulsen to unleash the speed of Jesper Grønkjær and Dennis Rommedahl on the wings.

Daniel Agger is a reliable defender for Liverpool, and Arsenal fans know all about the attacking skills of the tall and powerful Nicklas Bendtner. Both are products of Olsen's insistence on youth coaching and talent that has been nurtured in Danish national youth teams. Whatever happens, this is Olsen's last World Cup in charge – he will retire in 2010 so expectations are high.

Denmark v Sweden, World Cup Qualifier, Rasunda Stadium, Stockholm, 06.06.2009

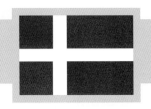

ROUTE TO THE FINALS

EUROPE QUALIFYING FINAL GROUP 1 – FINAL TABLE

TEAM	P	W	D	L	F	A	PTS
DENMARK	10	6	3	1	16	5	21
PORTUGAL	10	5	4	1	17	5	19
SWEDEN	10	5	3	2	13	5	18
HUNGARY	10	5	1	4	10	8	16
ALBANIA	10	1	4	5	6	13	7
MALTA	10	0	1	9	0	26	1

FINALS GROUP E

DENMARK PLAY	COUNTRY	DATE	VENUE
	NETHERLANDS	14.06.10	JOHANNESBURG - JSC
	CAMEROON	19.06.10	TSHWANE/ PRETORIA
	JAPAN	24.06.10	RUSTENBURG

VITAL STATISTICS

WORLD RANKING 26th
KEEPER AND DEFENCE 6/10
MIDFIELD 6/10
ATTACK 6/10

55

© Getty Images, Inc.

Japan v Australia, World Cup Qualifier,
Melbourne Cricket Ground, Melbourne, 17.06.2009

Having won the Asian Cup three times, Japan is now looking forward to their fourth World Cup Finals in a row. However, Japan's long-term form on the global stage suggests that significant progress beyond the opening rounds would be a big surprise.

There will be goalkeeping heroics from the veteran captain Seigo Narazaki, solid and gritty defensive displays led by Yuji Nakazawa, and there will be pace in attack. However, goals are always a problem for Japan – qualification relied on strong defence in 1–0 victories over Uzbekistan and Bahrain.

If Japan is to realise the hopes raised by its solid record, much will rely on the correct deployment of striker Shunsuke Nakamura's talents, and a more attack-minded 4-3-3 formation from new manager Takeshi Okada.

ROUTE TO THE FINALS

ASIA QUALIFYING FINAL GROUP 1 – FINAL TABLE

TEAM	P	W	D	L	F	A	PTS
AUSTRALIA	8	6	2	0	12	1	20
JAPAN	8	4	3	1	11	6	15
BAHRAIN	8	3	1	4	6	8	10
QATAR	8	1	3	4	5	14	6
UZBEKISTAN	8	1	1	6	5	10	4

FINALS GROUP E

JAPAN PLAY	COUNTRY	DATE	VENUE
	CAMEROON	14.06.10	MANGAUNG / BLOEMFONTEIN
	NETHERLANDS	19.06.10	DURBAN
	DENMARK	24.06.10	RUSTENBURG

VITAL STATISTICS
WORLD RANKING 43rd
KEEPER AND DEFENCE 6/10
MIDFIELD 5/10
ATTACK 4/10

CAMEROON

Cameroon was the first African team to reach the World Cup Quarter-finals (in 1990) and their success introduced the world to Roger Milla's talent.

Milla was the face of African football at the time, playing on into his forties, and it was a veteran side that faced the early qualifying rounds for South Africa 2010, managing just one point after two matches. A new manager, Paul Le Guen, a French import who started work in July 2009 appointed Samuel Eto'o as captain in place of the veteran defender Rigobert Song. In another move, Le Guen brought on an entirely new face, putting the 19-year-old Nicolas N'Koulou in defence for the emphatic 2–0 win against Morocco that sealed qualification.

Aside from the free-scoring Eto'o, Cameroon's big-name European exports put in well-muscled performances. Le Guen's run of four successive victories means Cameroon could prove surprising in South Africa.

Cameroon v Morocco, World Cup Qualifier, Complexe Sportif, Fes, 14.11.2009

ROUTE TO THE FINALS

AFRICA QUALIFYING GROUP A – FINAL TABLE

TEAM	P	W	D	L	F	A	PTS
CAMEROON	6	4	1	1	9	2	13
GABON	6	3	0	3	9	7	9
TOGO	6	2	2	2	3	7	8
MOROCCO	6	0	3	3	3	8	3

FINALS GROUP E

CAMEROON PLAY	COUNTRY	DATE	VENUE
	JAPAN	14.06.10	MANGAUNG / BLOEMFONTEIN
	DENMARK	19.06.10	TSHWANE/ PRETORIA
	NETHERLANDS	24.06.10	CAPE TOWN

VITAL STATISTICS
WORLD RANKING 11th
KEEPER AND DEFENCE 6/10
MIDFIELD 5/10
ATTACK 5/10

© Getty Images, Inc.

Italy v Bulgaria, World Cup Qualifier,
Olimpico Stadium, Turin, 09.09.2009

The current World Cup holders belong in the formidable Italian tradition of fielding teams that perform consistently at the top level. The Squadra Azzurra has been at 14 of the 16 World Cup Finals and has succeeded in lifting the cup in 1934, 1938, 1982 and 2006. Only Brazil has done better.

The enduring paradox of Italian sides is that they feature teamwork above individual talent and yet also accommodate individual brilliance. Successive well-drilled teams always know how to stifle the opposition. At the 2006 World Cup, Gianluigi Buffon, the 'keeper, was unbeaten for seven and a half hours of play. Italy conceded only two goals, one an own goal by Cristian Zaccardo and the second from Zinédine Zidane's penalty kick for France in the 1–1 stalemate of a Final match.

Members of this Italian squad understand each other's playing styles because many play together in Serie A, plus the reappointment of World Cup-winning manager, Marcello Lippi inspires confidence in an already bold team.

The final part of the recipe for success is that the team is kept on its toes as youth is constantly mixed in with experience.

ROUTE TO THE FINALS

EUROPE QUALIFYING FINAL GROUP 8 – FINAL TABLE

TEAM	P	W	D	L	F	A	PTS
ITALY	10	7	3	0	18	7	24
REPUBLIC OF IRELAND	10	4	6	0	12	8	18
BULGARIA	10	3	5	2	17	13	14
CYPRUS	10	2	3	4	14	16	9
MONTENEGRO	10	1	6	3	9	14	9
GEORGIA	10	0	3	7	7	19	3

FINALS GROUP F

ITALY

ITALY PLAY	COUNTRY	DATE	VENUE
	PARAGUAY	14.06.10	CAPE TOWN
	NEW ZEALAND	20.06.10	NELSPRUIT
	SLOVAKIA	24.06.10	JOHANNESBURG - JEP

VITAL STATISTICS

WORLD RANKING 4th
KEEPER AND DEFENCE 8/10
MIDFIELD 8/10
ATTACK 7/10

PARAGUAY

Paraguay's route to qualification for their fourth consecutive World Cup Finals saw an initial surge to the head of their South American group above Brazil, only to lose ground with one point from a possible 12 during the first half of 2009. They then outgunned more fancied rivals and booked a place to South Africa courtesy of a 1–0 defeat of Argentina.

In 2007 Gerardo 'Tata' Martino became the national manager charged with rejuvenating an ageing squad. He has built on youth team successes from earlier in the decade, and his remoulded side relies on the tested attacking skills of Cabañas, Valdez and Santa Cruz. Together, they have maintained Paraguay's reputation in South America for sound defence, aerial ability and powerfully built attackers.

Paraguay v Argentina, World Cup Qualifier,
Defensores del Chaco Stadium, Asuncion, 09.09.2009

ROUTE TO THE FINALS

SOUTH AMERICA QUALIFYING GROUP – FINAL TABLE

TEAM	P	W	D	L	F	A	PTS
BRAZIL	18	9	7	2	33	11	34
CHILE	18	10	3	5	32	22	33
PARAGUAY	18	10	3	5	24	16	33
ARGENTINA	18	8	4	6	23	20	28
URUGUAY	18	6	6	6	28	20	24
ECUADOR	18	6	5	7	22	26	23
COLOMBIA	18	6	5	7	14	18	23
VENEZUELA	18	6	4	8	23	29	22
BOLIVIA	18	4	3	11	22	36	15
PERU	18	3	4	11	11	34	13

FINALS GROUP F

PARAGUAY

PARAGUAY PLAY	COUNTRY	DATE	VENUE
	ITALY	14.06.10	CAPE TOWN
	SLOVAKIA	20.06.10	MANGAUNG / BLOEMFONTEIN
	NEW ZEALAND	24.06.10	POLOKWANE

VITAL STATISTICS

WORLD RANKING 30th
KEEPER AND DEFENCE 6/10
MIDFIELD 5/10
ATTACK 6/10

© Getty Images, Inc.

New Zealand v Bahrain, World Cup play-off, Westpac Stadium, Wellington, 14.11.2009

New Zealand had an easier route to South Africa than any of the other 31 participants. They didn't even have to meet Australia, who were transferred to the harder Asian group. Instead, New Zealand competed among Pacific tiddlers before beating Bahrain in a two-leg play-off that was settled by a single Rory Fallon headed goal.

Five clean sheets during qualification plus a Mark Paston penalty save in the second game against Bahrain all suggest a defensive resilience. Still, World Cup attendance is in itself some achievement for a nation where the main sporting draws are cricket and rugby.

Fans of the underdog will be rooting for New Zealand in 2010 – they are the rank outsiders with odds to win of 750-1 so an early exit seems likely despite their pluck.

ROUTE TO THE FINALS

OCEANIA QUALIFYING ROUND 2 – FINAL TABLE

TEAM	P	W	D	L	F	A	PTS
NEW ZEALAND	6	5	0	1	14	5	15
NEW CALEDONIA	6	2	2	2	12	10	8
FIJI	6	2	1	3	8	11	7
VANUATU	6	1	1	4	5	13	4

ASIA/OCEANIA PLAY-OFF

BAHRAIN	0	0	NEW ZEALAND
NEW ZEALAND	1	0	BAHRAIN

FINALS GROUP F

NEW ZEALAND PLAY	COUNTRY	DATE	VENUE
	SLOVAKIA	15.06.10	RUSTENBURG
	ITALY	20.06.10	NELSPRUIT
	PARAGUAY	24.06.10	POLOKWANE

VITAL STATISTICS

WORLD RANKING 77th
KEEPER AND DEFENCE 5/10
MIDFIELD 3/10
ATTACK 4/10

SLOVAKIA

Slovakia's qualification for South Africa is one of the surprises of the 2010 tournament. Since Czechoslovakia became two nations in 1993, Slovakia have qualified for nothing while the Czechs were at the 2006 World Cup, the Euro 96 Final and the Euro 2004 Semi-final.

Slovakia emerged from a tough qualifying group that lined them up against more fancied neighbours in the Czech Republic and Poland. In April 2009, they consolidated an unlikely position at the top of Group 3 by winning 2–1 on a visit to the Czech Republic. The praise went to the manager Vladimír Weiss, who has instilled discipline and belief into players who, while good enough to play throughout Europe, have failed to be rewarded with personal and national recognition. South Africa could change that.

© Getty Images, Inc.

Slovakia v Northern Ireland, World Cup Qualifier, Windsor Park, Belfast, 09.09.2009

ROUTE TO THE FINALS

EUROPE QUALIFYING GROUP 3 – FINAL TABLE

TEAM	P	W	D	L	F	A	PTS
SLOVAKIA	10	7	1	2	22	10	22
SLOVENIA	10	6	2	2	18	4	20
CZECH REPUBLIC	10	4	4	2	17	6	16
NORTHERN IRELAND	10	4	3	3	13	9	15
POLAND	10	3	2	5	19	14	11
SAN MARINO	10	0	0	10	1	47	0

FINALS GROUP F

SLOVAKIA PLAY	COUNTRY	DATE	VENUE
	NEW ZEALAND	15.06.10	RUSTENBURG
	PARAGUAY	20.06.10	MANGAUNG / BLOEMFONTEIN
	ITALY	24.06.10	JOHANNESBURG - JEP

VITAL STATISTICS

WORLD RANKING 34th
KEEPER AND DEFENCE 6/10
MIDFIELD 5/10
ATTACK 5/10

BRAZIL

© Getty Images, Inc.

Brazil v Spain, Confederations Cup Semi-final.
Ellis Park, Johannesburg, 25.06.2009

The world's best side plays the most beautiful version of the world's favourite sport. After being eliminated in the Quarter-finals in 2006, nothing less than a sixth title win will be good enough for Brazil.

Brazil's footballing record is awe inspiring. They were World Cup winners in 1958, 1962, 1970, 1994 and 2002 and have the unique achievement of having played in every World Cup. It is a mystery how each decade produces yet another clutch of star Brazilian players who meld their skills into stellar teams.

Current manager Dunga himself had the nerve to have scored in a World Cup Final penalty shoot-out, and the team have responded to an approach putting teamwork above individuality. A certain ruthlessness distinguishes this team from earlier Brazilian sides

and players take to the field with the confidence of those playing to a tested game plan. They are set up in a classic Brazilian counter-attacking and set-piece format that sometimes concedes possession to lure the opposition into complacency, and it's a tribute to Dunga's management that his side won the 2007 Copa América and the Confederations Cup in 2009.

Brazil are favourites for the 2010 World Cup, though tough competition will come from a resurgent Holland, a confident Spain or England, the sturdily constant threats of Italy and Germany plus France, Brazil's nemesis team. Although none will relish the prospect of facing Brazil in a penalty shoot-out – their record is unsurpassed.

ROUTE TO THE FINALS

SOUTH AMERICA QUALIFYING GROUP – FINAL TABLE

TEAM	P	W	D	L	F	A	PTS
BRAZIL	18	9	7	2	33	11	34
CHILE	18	10	3	5	32	22	33
PARAGUAY	18	10	3	5	24	16	33
ARGENTINA	18	8	4	6	23	20	28
URUGUAY	18	6	6	6	28	20	24
ECUADOR	18	6	5	7	22	26	23
COLOMBIA	18	6	5	7	14	18	23
VENEZUELA	18	6	4	8	23	29	22
BOLIVIA	18	4	3	11	22	36	15
PERU	18	3	4	11	11	34	13

FINALS GROUP G

BRAZIL

BRAZIL PLAY	COUNTRY	DATE	VENUE
	KOREA DPR	15.06.10	JOHANNESBURG - JEP
	CÔTE D'IVOIRE	20.06.10	JOHANNESBURG - JSC
	PORTUGAL	25.06.10	DURBAN

VITAL STATISTICS

WORLD RANKING 2nd
KEEPER AND DEFENCE 8/10
MIDFIELD 9/10
ATTACK 9/10

KOREA DPR

The North Korean team firmly established itself in British football folklore when heroic defending earned a place in the final eight of the 1966 World Cup. 2010 is Korea DPR's first World Cup Finals appearance since then.

Defence remains the team's watchword and the Democratic People's Republic of Korea (Korea DPR) had an impressive defensive record during qualifying stages. The goalkeeper Ri Myong-Guk provides backing for a rank of competent outfield stoppers; he is a clean-sheet specialist who did not let in a goal during four out of five of the last qualifying games.

The current Korea DPR team consists of home-grown players along with a few Zainichi Koreans who were brought up in Japan. Ahn Yong-Hak, the best known of these Japan-influenced players, is a versatile midfielder who will play a key role in South Africa.

© Getty Images, Inc.

Korea DPR v Korea Republic, World Cup Qualifier, World Cup Stadium, Seoul, 01.04.2009

ROUTE TO THE FINALS

ASIA QUALIFYING FINAL GROUP 2 – FINAL TABLE

TEAM	P	W	D	L	F	A	PTS
KOREA REPUBLIC	8	4	4	0	12	4	16
KOREA DPR	8	3	3	2	7	5	12
SAUDI ARABIA	8	3	3	2	8	8	12
IRAN	8	2	5	1	8	7	11
UNITED ARAB EMIRATES	8	0	1	7	6	17	1

FINALS GROUP G

KOREA DPR

KOREA DPR PLAY	COUNTRY	DATE	VENUE
	BRAZIL	15.06.10	JOHANNESBURG - JEP
	PORTUGAL	21.06.10	CAPE TOWN
	CÔTE D'IVOIRE	25.06.10	NELSPRUIT

VITAL STATISTICS

WORLD RANKING 84th
KEEPER AND DEFENCE 5/10
MIDFIELD 5/10
ATTACK 3/10

CÔTE D'IVOIRE

© Getty Images, Inc.

Côte d'Ivoire v Turkey, International friendly, Izmir Ataturk Stadium, Izmir, 11.02.2009

Côte d'Ivoire are Africa's best hope, with a cadre of players that would make it into many international squads. Any team would fear Kolo Touré at centre-back, Yaya Touré and Emmanuel Eboué in defensive midfield, and Salomon Kalou and Didier Drogba in attack.

Aside from qualifying for two World Cup Finals in a row, the greatest achievement was winning the 1992 African Cup of Nations… so far. However, the 2006 consensus is that they were a useful side that would have gone to the second round if they hadn't been in a tough group with Argentina and the Netherlands. They lost both games 2–1, which makes them the only team to have scored in all World Cup matches

they have participated in. If they do reach the later stages, their penalty shoot-out record reveals a team resilience in winning international football's two highest-scoring penalty shoot-outs: 11–10 against Ghana in the 1992 African Cup Final; and 12–11 in the 2006 African Cup Quarter-final.

They enter the World Cup Finals as the highest-ranking team in Africa, and hopes are high, now that the stuttering progress in Qualifiers against Burkina Faso, Guinea and Malawi is behind them. During those games, the defensive midfield remained strong, but if they hope to progress in South Africa they need to get the ball to Salomon Kalou and Didier Drogba in attack.

ROUTE TO THE FINALS

AFRICA QUALIFYING GROUP E – FINAL TABLE

TEAM	P	W	D	L	F	A	PTS
CÔTE D'IVOIRE	6	5	1	0	19	4	16
BURKINA FASO	6	4	0	2	10	11	12
MALAWI	6	1	1	4	4	11	4
GUINEA	6	1	0	5	7	14	3

FINALS GROUP G

CÔTE D'IVOIRE PLAY	COUNTRY	DATE	VENUE
	PORTUGAL	15.06.10	NELSON MANDELA BAY/PORT ELIZABETH
	BRAZIL	20.06.10	JOHANNESBURG - JSC
	KOREA DPR	25.06.10	NELSPRUIT

VITAL STATISTICS

WORLD RANKING 16th
KEEPER AND DEFENCE 7/10
MIDFIELD 5/10
ATTACK 8/10

73

PORTUGAL

Portugal's past record is formidable. The Selecção das Quinas eliminated England from Euro 2004 and from the last World Cup. They made the Finals of Euro 2004, and reached their second World Cup Semi-final in 2006.

Big acts are hard to follow and many big names of that era have retired. Gone too is Phil Scolari, whose replacement, Carlos Queiroz, has a big problem. Although he can field the best player in the world, it will only be in a team that struggled to qualify.

There are other flashes of talent though – Eduardo's goalkeeping prowess rocketed him from zero to hero in an international career trajectory that began when he was 26. From February 2009, Eduardo let in only two goals in eleven matches enabling Portugal to edge away from 2010 World Cup oblivion.

But the reason many people welcome Portugal's qualification is Cristiano Ronaldo, who was unavailable for Portugal's later qualifying games due to injury. Ronaldo's raw skill was refined at Manchester United when Queiroz was Sir Alex Ferguson's assistant, and the two ensured he matured into the best player in the world. There's a tactical sympathy between manager and a remarkable player who, at 25, is in his prime and looking to carve an international career which will secure his place in history.

Portugal v Bosnia-Herzegovina, World Cup Qualifier,
Luz Stadium, Lisbon, 14.11.2009

ROUTE TO THE FINALS

EUROPE QUALIFYING GROUP 1 – FINAL TABLE

TEAM	P	W	D	L	F	A	PTS
DENMARK	10	6	3	1	16	5	21
PORTUGAL	10	5	4	1	17	5	19
SWEDEN	10	5	3	2	13	5	18
HUNGARY	10	5	1	4	10	8	16
ALBANIA	10	1	4	5	6	13	7
MALTA	10	0	1	9	0	26	1

EUROPE PLAY-OFFS

PORTUGAL	1	0	BOSNIA-HERZEGOVINA
BOSNIA-HERZEGOVINA	0	1	PORTUGAL

FINALS GROUP G

PORTUGAL

PORTUGAL PLAY	COUNTRY	DATE	VENUE
	CÔTE D'IVOIRE	15.06.10	NELSON MANDELA BAY/PORT ELIZABETH
	KOREA DPR	21.06.10	CAPE TOWN
	BRAZIL	25.06.10	DURBAN

VITAL STATISTICS

WORLD RANKING 5th
KEEPER AND DEFENCE 7/10
MIDFIELD 6/10
ATTACK 8/10

SPAIN

© Getty Images, Inc.

Spain v Germany, Euro 2008 Final,
Ernst Happel Stadion, Vienna, 29.06.2008

Both Spain and England can look back on unlucky Quarter-final defeats, poor refereeing and lost penalty shoot-outs in previous World Cups. But in the run-up to South Africa 2010, both sides sailed through the Qualifiers – both of them, incidentally, under managers who had led Real Madrid to championship medals in La Liga (England manager Fabio Capello in 2007 and Spanish manager Vicente del Bosque in 2001 and 2003). Spain under del Bosque dominated their qualifying group, with a perfect 10 victories against Bosnia-Herzegovina, Turkey, Armenia, Estonia and Belgium.

Del Bosque can select a squad with deep experience in the world's two top leagues – the Spanish La Liga and the English Premiership. He is popular with established players, and rather than giving lectures to the experienced, he allows them to express their talents. And there is talent in abundance.

In goal, Spain is spoilt for choice with Real Madrid's Iker Casillas vying with Liverpool's Pepe Reina. Sergio Ramos will dominate defence. The midfield is crowded with playmakers and one of the big questions of the 2010 World Cup is whether or not Arsenal's Cesc Fàbregas will be given the chance to play a truly creative role alongside Barcelona's Andrés Iniesta. Perhaps the answer has to do with del Bosque, whose time at Real Madrid had him fully exploiting the talents of Luís Figo, Zinédine Zidane and Ronaldo. The players del Bosque will have to drop would be definites for most other international teams and with talent like that, this time Spain could go all the way.

ROUTE TO THE FINALS

EUROPE QUALIFYING GROUP 5 – FINAL TABLE

TEAM	P	W	D	L	F	A	PTS
SPAIN	10	10	0	0	28	5	30
BOSNIA-HERZEGOVINA	10	6	1	3	25	13	19
TURKEY	10	4	3	3	13	10	15
BELGIUM	10	3	1	6	13	20	10
ESTONIA	10	2	2	6	9	24	8
ARMENIA	10	1	1	8	6	22	4

FINALS GROUP H

SPAIN PLAY	COUNTRY	DATE	VENUE
	SWITZERLAND	16.06.10	DURBAN
	HONDURAS	21.06.10	JOHANNESBURG - JEP
	CHILE	25.06.10	TSHWANE/PRETORIA

VITAL STATISTICS

WORLD RANKING 1st
KEEPER AND DEFENCE 9/10
MIDFIELD 8/10
ATTACK 8/10

SWITZERLAND

When Switzerland drew 0–0 at home to Israel to gain World Cup qualification, the nation looked back on previous World Cup Quarter-final appearances in 1934, 1938 and 1954.

The Swiss team famously struggle with goals, but do, however, boast a star attraction: Ottmar Hitzfeld, a manager of exceptional pedigree. Hitzfeld has won 18 trophies at club level, was elected FIFA Coach of the Year in 1997 and 2001, and is one of only two managers to have won the Champions League with two clubs, Borussia Dortmund and Bayern Munich.

His fighting spirit has turned a lacklustre side into a coherent, hard-working and efficient unit.

The Swiss captain, Alexander Frei is the nation's top scorer with 40 goals. He will muster troops who are strongest in a defence marshalled by Arsenal's Philippe Senderos. Hitzfeld will hope that age and injury won't prevent Hakan Yakin and Bayer Leverkusen's Tranquillo Barnetta from patrolling midfield. After that, it's down to teamwork, and there's arguably no better touchline organiser than Ottmar Hitzfeld.

Switzerland v Greece, World Cup Qualifier,
St. Jakob-Park Stadium, Basel, 05.09.2009

ROUTE TO THE FINALS

EUROPE QUALIFYING GROUP 2 – FINAL TABLE

TEAM	P	W	D	L	F	A	PTS
SWITZERLAND	10	6	3	1	18	8	21
GREECE	10	6	2	2	20	10	20
LATVIA	10	5	2	3	18	15	17
ISRAEL	10	4	4	2	20	10	16
LUXEMBOURG	10	1	2	7	4	25	5
MOLDOVA	10	0	3	7	6	18	3

FINALS GROUP H

SWITZERLAND PLAY	COUNTRY	DATE	VENUE
	SPAIN	16.06.10	DURBAN
	CHILE	21.06.10	NELSON MANDELA BAY/PORT ELIZABETH
	HONDURAS	25.06.10	MANGAUNG / BLOEMFONTEIN

VITAL STATISTICS

WORLD RANKING 18th
KEEPER AND DEFENCE 6/10
MIDFIELD 5/10
ATTACK 4/10

HONDURAS

© Getty Images, Inc.

*Honduras v El Salvador, World Cup Qualifier,
Estadio Cuscatlàn, San Salvador, 14.10.2009*

The Hondurans' 1–0 win in El Salvador seemed in vain because their rivals, Costa Rica, were still playing and were ahead in a game that would have relegated Honduras to the play-offs. Then came an injury-time equaliser against Costa Rica and the instant creation of two heroes: Honduras's own Carlos Pavón for scoring in El Salvador and the USA's Jonathan Bornstein for equalising in Costa Rica.

Honduras has several players who are worth watching. The best known in Europe is Inter Milan's David Suazo, also known as 'the Panther', whose pace and inventiveness in front of goal were missed during the qualification struggle due to injuries. Another one to watch is Wilson Palacios, whose intelligent distribution impressed Wigan fans before he moved on to Tottenham Hotspur.

Reinaldo Rueda, a Colombian disciplinarian who has managed Honduras since 2006, has prepared a side that mixes youth with age, skill with organisation. Much is expected of the first national side to make it to the World Cup Finals since 1982 and, after the hysteria accompanying the last-gasp qualification, Honduran football fever runs high.

ROUTE TO THE FINALS

CONCACAF FINAL STAGE – FINAL TABLE

TEAM	P	W	D	L	F	A	PTS
USA	10	6	2	2	19	13	20
MEXICO	10	6	1	3	18	12	19
HONDURAS	10	5	1	4	17	11	16
COSTA RICA	10	5	1	4	15	15	16
EL SALVADOR	10	2	2	6	9	15	8
TRINIDAD & TOBAGO	10	1	3	6	10	22	6

FINALS GROUP H

HONDURAS PLAY	COUNTRY	DATE	VENUE
	CHILE	16.06.10	NELSPRUIT
	SPAIN	21.06.10	JOHANNESBURG - JEP
	SWITZERLAND	25.06.10	MANGAUNG / BLOEMFONTEIN

VITAL STATISTICS
WORLD RANKING 38th
KEEPER AND DEFENCE 5/10
MIDFIELD 6/10
ATTACK 5/10

CHILE

Chile's triumphant qualification campaign included their first ever point playing Uruguay in Montevideo; a 1–0 win over Argentina precipitated the resignation of the Argentine coach Alfio Basile; and away victories were secured in Peru and Paraguay.

A campaign such as that might be expected of one of the 13 nations to have taken part in the inaugural 1930 World Cup and a further six World Cups, and new manager, Marcelo Bielsa, has been the driving force behind the new Chile. He played his football as a defender and found fame as manager of his native Argentina for six years. Bielsa, has stabilized a fractious Chile squad that shortly before his appointment in 2007 had banned six senior players for 'internal indiscipline' during the Copa América tournament. This forced a rapid adoption of youthful players, whom Bielsa has deployed in attacking formations, notably away from home. Thorough preparation and intelligent tactical flexibility secured the famous run of qualifying results.

South America has rocked to Bielsa's Chilean renaissance and unleashed a style of play that might just lighten Chile's reputation. The major talent to have prospered under the new regime is Mark González, a pacy left-winger and the most-capped player in the current squad.

Chile v Brazil, World Cup Qualifier, Pituacu Stadium, Santiago, 09.09.2009

ROUTE TO THE FINALS

SOUTH AMERICA QUALIFYING GROUP – FINAL TABLE

TEAM	P	W	D	L	F	A	PTS
BRAZIL	18	9	7	2	33	11	34
CHILE	18	10	3	5	32	22	33
PARAGUAY	18	10	3	5	24	16	33
ARGENTINA	18	8	4	6	23	20	28
URUGUAY	18	6	6	6	28	20	24
ECUADOR	18	6	5	7	22	26	23
COLOMBIA	18	6	5	7	14	18	23
VENEZUELA	18	6	4	8	23	29	22
BOLIVIA	18	4	3	11	22	36	15
PERU	18	3	4	11	11	34	13

FINALS GROUP H

CHILE PLAY	COUNTRY	DATE	VENUE
	HONDURAS	16.06.10	NELSPRUIT
	SWITZERLAND	21.06.10	NELSON MANDELA BAY/PORT ELIZABETH
	SPAIN	25.06.10	TSHWANE/PRETORIA

VITAL STATISTICS
WORLD RANKING 17th
KEEPER AND DEFENCE 6/10
MIDFIELD 5/10
ATTACK 5/10

JOHN TERRY
ENGLAND

FACT FILE
NAME John Terry
POSITION Defender
CAPS 58
GOALS 6
CLUB Chelsea
DATE OF BIRTH 07.12.1980
HEIGHT 184 cm
WEIGHT 88 kg
PREVIOUS CLUBS None
INTERNATIONAL DEBUT 03.06.2003 v Serbia and Montenegro
PREVIOUS WORLD CUPS 2006

John Terry is an inspirational and highly effective centre-back. He was made Chelsea captain at 23, having served an apprenticeship in defensive arts when playing alongside the French World Cup-winning pair of Marcel Desailly and Frank Leboeuf. He led Chelsea to two Premier League titles in 2004–05 with the most clean sheets and the best defensive record in league history. That season he scored eight goals, including a late winner against Barcelona in the Champions League.

He made his full international debut in a friendly against Croatia in 2003. England won the game 3–1 and his main defensive partner in the victory was Rio Ferdinand. It was the beginning of an enduring international partnership that makes the English defence one of the most feared in the world. With these two players in their prime, and with both anticipating South Africa 2010 as their last chance of an England Final, opportunity and motivation could not be higher.

PLAYING STYLE

Faultless is the word that often crops up in reports of matches in which John Terry has taken part. He is a rugged centre-back whose influence extends beyond his powerful tackle, his heading ability, his understanding of the game and his upfield forays for free kicks and corners, encouraging through force of example.

84

FACT FILE

NAME Rio Ferdinand
POSITION Defender
CAPS 76
GOALS 3
CLUB Manchester United
DATE OF BIRTH 07.11.1978
HEIGHT 188 cm
WEIGHT 77 kg
PREVIOUS CLUBS Leeds United, Bournemouth (loan), West Ham United
INTERNATIONAL DEBUT 15.11.1997 v Cameroon
PREVIOUS WORLD CUPS 2006, 2002

Rio Ferdinand played in the 2002 and 2006 World Cup Finals and his experience at every level of the game is underpinned with a blend of composure and speed. It's no surprise that he has been one of the first names on the England team-sheet for the best part of a decade.

When needs must, Ferdinand is a traditional stopper who will give strikers a tough time, then fire the ball upfield to clear his lines. However, his more cultured technique is what distinguishes him and his ability to make the telling pass helps England play the international game of building from the back. He will also pop up in the box at set pieces to knock in the odd goal as he did in the World Cup qualifying game against Kazakhstan.

Ferdinand was barely 19 when he got his first full England cap as a substitute in a friendly against Cameroon in 1997. He developed at West Ham and Leeds and joined Manchester United in July 2002 where he has helped his club to five Premiership firsts and one Champions League title.

South Africa is probably the last chance for Ferdinand to cement his reputation as the world's best, and he will be aiming to make 11 July 2010 the day when Rio Ferdinand adds an England World Cup winners' medal to the hatful of league and cup medals he has already earned.

PLAYING STYLE

Tactically astute and, injury permitting, athletically mobile, Rio Ferdinand is the complete modern centre-back. Team awareness reinforces his attributes and he forms outstanding partnerships with the likes of Nemanja Vidić for Manchester United. The current pairing of Ferdinand and Terry makes this England central defence a rock on which most attacks will founder.

FACT FILE

NAME Wayne Rooney
POSITION Striker
CAPS 57
GOALS 25
CLUB Manchester United
DATE OF BIRTH 24.10.1985
HEIGHT 178 cm
WEIGHT 81 kg
PREVIOUS CLUB Everton
INTERNATIONAL DEBUT 12.02.2003 v Australia
PREVIOUS WORLD CUPS 2006

The hopes of a nation rest on Wayne Rooney's muscular young shoulders. He is the undisputed English footballer of his generation and with Rooney on form, England is a serious contender for World Cup glory.

Rooney's strength and balance achieve an odd grace and his sheer physicality animates team-mates and crowds alike. His exciting talent and extraordinary energy have illuminated so many big games, it's hard to credit that he's not yet 25. Despite relentless press exposure and unremitting pressures of expectation, Rooney's will to win seems as fresh as when he made his England debut against Australia in 2003 and then quickly emerged as the star of Euro 2004.

An injured foot marred Rooney's (and England's) chances of significant World Cup progress in 2006. Four years ago, the nation became experts on broken metatarsals while Rooney struggled for fitness. Rooney was on less-than-peak form as England laboured towards a Quarter-final clash with Portugal where he was sent off after a controversial confrontation with Cristiano Ronaldo. England eventually went out on penalties.

An older, wiser Rooney will be looking to redeem himself in South Africa. With three Premier League titles and the 2008 Champions League among his club honours, he is already an Old Trafford legend where he wears the number 10 shirt. For England he has the same number and it is likely that in South Africa he will stay up front in the spearhead role and go flat out to score.

PLAYING STYLE

Rooney rides tackles bravely to terrify defences with rollicking runs into shooting positions. The passing and the movement are clever too. His control at speed is phenomenal, he has the wit to pull off the trickiest of lobs and the power to volley with either foot.

FACT FILE

NAME Steven Gerrard
POSITION Midfielder
CAPS 77
GOALS 16
CLUB Liverpool
DATE OF BIRTH 30.05.1980
HEIGHT 183 cm
WEIGHT 78 kg
PREVIOUS CLUBS None
INTERNATIONAL DEBUT 31.05.2000 v Ukraine
PREVIOUS WORLD CUPS 2006

There are few better sights in football than Steven Gerrard marshalling an attack and mixing astute prodded passes with raking cross-fielders. And all the while is the exciting possibility that he'll find the net himself, as he showed at the last World Cup when he was England's top scorer.

Gerrard is a one-club man who has played in just about every position for Liverpool and scored in four major Finals, something no other English player has done. He will make himself a national hero if he can do for England what he has done for his home town.

Especially worth noting is the way he led Liverpool's comeback against AC Milan in the 2005 Champions League Final. During a six-minute stretch in the second half, Liverpool clawed back a three-goal deficit to draw 3–3 after extra-time, with Gerrard scoring one of the goals. Liverpool's third goal was from a penalty after Gerrard was brought down in Milan's penalty box. The pressing question for England fans is can Steven Gerrard push forward to repeat something like this for England in South Africa?

The Lampard/Gerrard question is key and the pair need to prove they can mesh their centrally based forward-looking skills. That said, Gerrard is a big-game player with plenty of solid international experience, not least his impressive contributions during England's serene progress through the World Cup qualifying rounds.

PLAYING STYLE

Steven Gerrard has the will and the energy to drive a team to victory and the power and pace to go with a never-say-die attitude. He is versatile and most often used in central midfield, though he can drift right or left, or move up the pitch as an auxiliary striker. He needs a free role to play at his inspirational peak.

ENGLAND

ENGLAND

FACT FILE

NAME Frank Lampard
POSITION Midfielder
CAPS 76
GOALS 20
CLUB Chelsea
DATE OF BIRTH 20.06.1978
HEIGHT 183 cm
WEIGHT 88 kg
PREVIOUS CLUBS West Ham United, Swansea City (loan)
INTERNATIONAL DEBUT 10.10.1999 v Belgium
PREVIOUS WORLD CUPS 2006

Lampard's service record reveals a midfield strategist who, from commanding positions at the centre of the park, plays an elegant, unruffled game creating the time and space to initiate attacks. His goal scoring is an added extra, but was something that was always expected from the man who stepped into the England side as Paul Scholes' successor.

At Chelsea, Lampard is the local hero who has fired more goals for his club than any other midfielder. Internationally he started well, scoring nine for the England Under-21s, a tally only exceeded by Alan Shearer and Francis Jeffers. He got three goals in four matches as England made it to the Quarter-finals at Euro 2004, and fans voted him England Player of the Year in 2004 and 2005.

Then despite playing every minute of England's 2006 World Cup campaign, and shooting more frequently than any other England player, Lampard failed to score, and he took some of the blame when England failed to progress beyond the last eight.

When Fabio Capello took over the England managership in 2008, Lampard found himself playing international catch-up. He responded slowly but surely with his first international goal in two years in a 4–0 win over Slovakia in March 2009. Equally important was the assist for a Wayne Rooney goal. Now that Lampard is matching his international showings with those for Chelsea, the big question is how well he and Steven Gerrard can play in the World Cup.

PLAYING STYLE

Consistent and superbly fit, Frank Lampard is a goal-scoring midfielder with an accurate pass and a well-timed tackle. Despite the benefits of deploying him as an advanced attacking midfielder, managers like to exploit his stamina and usually instruct him to work as a box-to-box midfielder.

ASHLEY COLE

FACT FILE
NAME Ashley Cole
POSITION Defender
CAPS 77
GOALS 0
CLUB Chelsea
DATE OF BIRTH 20.12.1980
HEIGHT 173 cm
WEIGHT 67 kg
PREVIOUS CLUB Arsenal, Crystal Palace (loan)
INTERNATIONAL DEBUT 28.03.2001 v Albania
PREVIOUS WORLD CUPS 2002, 2006

In 2000 the young Ashley Cole pushed aside the Brazilian international Sylvinho to claim an Arsenal place. After a mere 19 Premiership appearances, he made his international debut in a World Cup Qualifier against Albania. The next year he also won his first FA Cup Final medal, something he went on to win a record five times. In 2003, he was a vital component of the Arsenal defence that lasted a whole Premiership campaign without losing a match. His selected highlights include a few goals as well, such as the one in 2003 against Dynamo Kiev that kept Arsenal in the Champions League, and the penalty shoot-out goal that secured a 2005 FA Cup medal against Manchester United.

Sven-Göran Eriksson played Cole in a win against Albania that helped take England through to Korea/Japan 2002. Cole played in every England game in the 2006 World Cup, then continued as a first choice on the team sheets during Steve McClaren's brief reign. His form and fitness have been maintained and he'll be a key figure in Fabio Capello's plans for South Africa 2010.

PLAYING STYLE
Consistent in the tackle and astute in positioning, Cole is the ultimate in efficient left-sided defenders.

FACT FILE

NAME David James
POSITION Goalkeeper
CAPS 49
GOALS 0
CLUB Portsmouth
DATE OF BIRTH 01.08.1970
HEIGHT 195 cm
WEIGHT 98 kg
PREVIOUS CLUBS INCLUDE
Manchester City, West Ham United,
Aston Villa, Liverpool, Watford
INTERNATIONAL DEBUT 29.03.1997
v Mexico
PREVIOUS WORLD CUPS 2002, 2006

On 6 February 2008, David James was picked for Fabio Capello's first match in charge and played his first full game in England's goal since 2005 – he kept a clean sheet. What might have impressed Capello was the way James consulted sports psychologists to give him the edge at penalty kicks. These things can make all the difference.

James's stop-start international career began with a friendly against Mexico in 1997. After David Seaman's final international in 2002, James became England's first choice. He played throughout Euro 2004 but was dropped later that year following an error in a 2–2 World Cup Qualifier against Austria. His lowest point came a year later as halftime substitute when he conceded all the goals in Denmark's 4–1 thrashing of England. But he has made more Premier League appearances than any other footballer, and has the most clean sheets in Premiership history. A couple of clean sheets could clinch it for England in South Africa and top off a distinguished career that Fabio Capello so wisely revived.

PLAYING STYLE

Athleticism and timing make David James unsurpassed as a shot-stopper. However, he is also known for rushing out of the goal when he should stay put. A recent spate of injuries and long recovery time between matches have all been of concern lately.

© PA Photos

THEO WALCOTT

ENGLAND

FACT FILE

NAME Theo Walcott
POSITION Striker
CAPS 8
GOALS 3
CLUB Arsenal
DATE OF BIRTH 16.03.1989
HEIGHT 175 cm
WEIGHT 68 kg
PREVIOUS CLUB Southampton
INTERNATIONAL DEBUT
30.05.2006 v Hungary
PREVIOUS WORLD CUPS 2006

Theo Walcott became England's youngest player aged 17 years 75 days in a 3–1 defeat of Hungary. By then, Sven-Göran Eriksson had included him in the 2006 World Cup squad as back-up to Wayne Rooney and Michael Owen. The choice was controversial but the teenage prodigy came good for Fabio Capello when, in 2008, he became the youngest England hat-trick scorer in the 4–1 win over Croatia in Zagreb.

At 15, he was Southampton's youngest ever reserve. He set another Southampton record when he joined the first team aged 16 years and 143 days. At the beginning of 2006, he went to Arsenal and the following August he made his Premiership debut in the first game at the new Emirates Stadium.

Walcott's status as national treasure elect was confirmed when he paraded around London carrying the Olympic flame for Beijing 2008. That parade would be as nothing compared to a 2010 World Cup victory cavalcade.

PLAYING STYLE

Walcott's blistering pace scares the defenders he runs at. When he cuts in from the right, goalkeepers quake in anticipation of powerful shots that leave them confused because they're delivered with so little backlift. If he goes to the byline, central defenders have grown wary of Walcott's accuracy with a cross.

96

© PA Photos

GARETH BARRY ENGLAND

FACT FILE

NAME Gareth Barry
POSITION Midfielder
CAPS 35
GOALS 2
CLUB Manchester City
DATE OF BIRTH 23.02.81
HEIGHT 183 cm
WEIGHT 79 kg
PREVIOUS CLUB Aston Villa
INTERNATIONAL DEBUT
31.05.00 v Ukraine
PREVIOUS WORLD CUPS None

Gareth Barry has the rare privilege of having played under five different England managers, and having won his first cap in 2000 he has been playing for England intermittently ever since.

In midfield, he forms a solid working partnership with fellow defender Steven Gerrard, but having fallen from favour during Sven-Göran Eriksson's time at the helm, Barry didn't make a single appearance for four years. It was Steve McClaren who offered Barry the second chance he needed, and he joined the team that faced, and eventually lost to, Spain at Old Trafford in February 2007.

His performance later that year during the November 2007 England v Estonia Qualifer for Euro 2008 saw him awarded Man of the Match for his part in the 3-0 England victory.

On top of this, Barry also takes full advantage of the opportunity to score goals, and has scored against Trinidad & Tobago, and in an early World Cup Qualifier against Kazakhstan in June 2009 heading a cross from Steven Gerrard to find the back of the net.

PLAYING STYLE

Barry's strong team-ethic and unselfish style provide a strong back-up for Lampard and Gerrard in midfield, as well as being able to weigh in with the odd goal.

MATTHEW UPSON

ENGLAND

FACT FILE

NAME Matthew Upson
POSITION Defender
CAPS 18
GOALS 1
CLUB West Ham United
DATE OF BIRTH 18.04.79
HEIGHT 185 cm
WEIGHT 72 kg
PREVIOUS CLUBS INCLUDE
Birmingham City, Arsenal, Luton Town
INTERNATIONAL DEBUT 22.05.03
v South Africa
PREVIOUS WORLD CUPS None

Matthew Upson was signed by Arsenal after just one appearance for his first club Luton Town. After making 56 appearances for the Gunners and picking up a Premier League winners' medal, Upson joined Birmingham in January 2003 before joining current club West Ham in January 2007.

Upson's impressive performances with previous club Birmingham City led to his first international call-up in May 2003 to face South Africa.

In February 2008, Fabio Capello called on Upson to once more play for the Three Lions in a friendly against Switzerland. A powerful partnership with Rio Ferdinand helped him to firmly establish his place at the heart of England's defence. He went on to feature in the last four internationals of that year.

Amongst this was his opportunity to replace an injured John Terry for the full 90 minutes during the World Cup Qualifier against Kazakhstan in October 2008.

Upson scored his first goal for England in November 2008 in a 2-1 victory over Germany in Berlin.

PLAYING STYLE

Guided by Fabio Capello and West Ham boss, Gianfranco Zola, Upson's confidence has soared. Now that he is enjoying more starts, the practice of facing the best players in the world has made Upson raise his game to match, and there's every chance he will play a big role in South Africa.

PETER CROUCH

FACT FILE

NAME Peter Crouch
POSITION Striker
CAPS 36
GOALS 18
CLUB Tottenham Hotspur
DATE OF BIRTH 30.01.81
HEIGHT 201 cm
WEIGHT 84 kg
PREVIOUS CLUBS INCLUDE
Portsmouth, Liverpool, Southampton
INTERNATIONAL DEBUT 31.05.05
v Colombia
PREVIOUS WORLD CUPS 2006

Scoring 17 goals in the 2004-05 season for previous club side Southampton, Peter Crouch earned a call-up for the USA Tour in May 2005.

He took his place in the England side in time for a pre-World Cup friendly against Hungary in May 2006, and scored the third goal of what became a 3-1 win.

Once again showing how deadly his skills and ability to exploit a weak defence can be, Crouch donned the Three Lions in another pre-World Cup friendly, this time against Jamaica. His hat-trick of goals helped England on to the final score of 6-0.

In 2008, Crouch switched clubs from Liverpool to FA Cup winners Portsmouth, and his performance in Euro 2008 Qualifiers made him the first England player to have scored 10 goals in a single calendar year.

During qualification for South Africa, Crouch once again shone. His first-half goal against Belarus in the final Qualifier was followed up with a second goal in the 74th minute giving him 18 goals in just 17 starts.

PLAYING STYLE

While he could form a partnership with other strikers, feeding balls to his strike partner, Crouch is a confident goalscorer in his own right and goes into every game believing he can score.

© Getty Images, Inc

FACT FILE

NAME Daniel Alves da Silva
POSITION Defender
CAPS 32
GOALS 3
CLUB Barcelona
DATE OF BIRTH 06.05.1983
HEIGHT 173 cm
WEIGHT 68 kg
PREVIOUS CLUBS
Bahia, Sevilla
INTERNATIONAL DEBUT
10.10.2006 v Ecuador
PREVIOUS WORLD CUPS
None

Daniel Alves is one of the best fullbacks in the world. He's also an attacker who sets off on swashbuckling upfield forays and who, during the moments of a game when Brazil are most likely to pounce, delivers an explosive free kick.

Alves is well known in Europe and had to endure the disappointment of missing the 2009 Champions League Final due to a yellow-card suspension. Before joining Barcelona, he spent six years at Sevilla where he won UEFA Super Cup, Copa del Rey, the Spanish Super Cup and two UEFA Cups.

He was a late arrival as an international superstar in the 2007 Copa América Final when he entered play as a substitute to set up Brazil's second goal and score their third in a 3–0 defeat of Argentina. He further enhanced his international standing as a substitute in the 2009 Confederations Cup Semi-final against South Africa. In the 88th minute he hit a free kick reminiscent of Roberto Carlos, to secure his side a 1–0 win and himself a more secure place in Brazil's international set-up.

One of the hardest-tackling fullbacks in the world, Alves' stamina and aggression make him tough to beat in defence.

NICOLAS ANELKA

FACT FILE
NAME Nicolas Sebastien Anelka
POSITION Striker
CAPS 63
GOALS 14
CLUB Chelsea
DATE OF BIRTH 14.03.1979
HEIGHT 183 cm
WEIGHT 77 kg
PREVIOUS CLUBS Paris St-Germain, Arsenal, Real Madrid, Paris St-Germain, Liverpool, Manchester City, Fenerbahçe, Bolton Wanderers
INTERNATIONAL DEBUT 22.04.1998 v Sweden
PREVIOUS WORLD CUPS None

© Getty Images, Inc.

In 1997, Arsenal's new manager, Arsène Wenger, snapped up the talented 17 year old. The next year France won the World Cup, Anelka was named French Young Footballer of the Year, he won the double with Arsenal and he made his international debut. Two years later Wenger sold his protégé to Real Madrid at a £20 million profit.

A previously unsettled Anelka finally settled at Chelsea in 2008 and was hailed as the French saviour as he (and France) hit form towards the end of the World Cup qualifying run. He scored the only goal to win the first play-off in the Republic of Ireland and will no doubt play a decisive role in South Africa.

FACT FILE
NAME Michael Ballack
POSITION Midfielder
CAPS 97
GOALS 42
CLUB Chelsea
DATE OF BIRTH 26.09.1976
HEIGHT 189 cm
WEIGHT 89 kg
PREVIOUS CLUBS Bayern Munich, Bayer Leverkusen, 1. FC Kaiserslautern, Chemnitzer FC
INTERNATIONAL DEBUT 28.04.1999 v Scotland
PREVIOUS WORLD CUPS 2002, 2006

© Getty Images, Inc.

GERMANY

Jürgen Klinsmann's first move as manager was to make Ballack captain, and he moulded the lesser talents available to him around his star midfielder. Joachim Löw maintained the approach and both managers have been rewarded with goals and match-winning leadership. Ballack is an all-rounder and the statistically superstitious will note that Germany has never lost a game when Ballack has scored.

MICHAEL BALLACK

ITALY

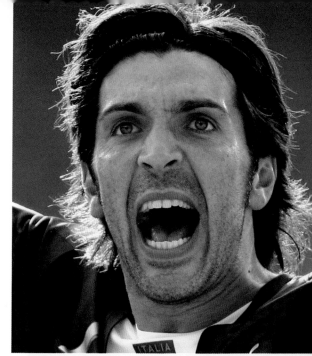

FACT FILE
NAME Gianluigi Buffon
POSITION Goalkeeper
CAPS 100
GOALS 0
CLUB Juventus
DATE OF BIRTH 28.01.1978
HEIGHT 191 cm
WEIGHT 83 kg
PREVIOUS CLUB Parma
INTERNATIONAL DEBUT
29.10.1997 v Russia
PREVIOUS WORLD CUPS 1998, 2002, 2006

© Getty Images, Inc.

Gianluigi Buffon is one of the greatest goalkeepers in the history of the game. He was awarded his first Italy cap at the age of 19 during a World Cup Qualifer play-off against Russia in 1998, and led Italy through Euro 2008 after injury ruled out Fabio Cannavaro as captain. He earned the UEFA Most Valuable Player and Best Goalkeeper awards in 2003, and during the 2006 World Cup Finals, Buffon kept five clean sheets and denied a goal to all attackers who faced him for an astonishing 453 minutes.

FACT FILE
NAME Tim Cahill
POSITION Midfielder
CAPS 37
GOALS 19
CLUB Everton
DATE OF BIRTH 06.12.1979
HEIGHT 178 cm
WEIGHT 68 kg
PREVIOUS CLUB Millwall
INTERNATIONAL DEBUT
30.03.2004 v South Africa
PREVIOUS WORLD CUPS 2006

© Getty Images, Inc.

A central midfielder and natural goal scorer, Tim Cahill is the most talented Australian footballer of this or any other generation, scoring the first ever Australia World Cup goal in a match against Japan in 2006.

Cahill spent the start of his club career at Millwall before moving to Everton at the end of 2007. That move saw him graduate to a more full-on attacker and he finished his first Premiership campaign as Everton's top scorer. South Africa beckons, and Cahill will be a fully fledged star on his 2010 trip.

TIM CAHILL

FACT FILE

NAME Fabio Cannavaro
POSITION Defender
CAPS 131
GOALS 2
CLUB Juventus
DATE OF BIRTH 13.09.1973
HEIGHT 176 cm
WEIGHT 75 kg
PREVIOUS CLUBS Napoli, Parma, Inter Milan, Juventus, Real Madrid
INTERNATIONAL DEBUT 22.01.1997 v Northern Ireland
PREVIOUS WORLD CUPS 1998, 2002, 2006

Can Italy's captain and most-capped player make it two in a row and take the Azzurri to victory in South Africa? Or will his fourth World Cup campaign prove to be one too many?

Despite age and a recent history of serious injury, Fabio Cannavaro has been quite open in his determination to captain Italy through the 2010 World Cup. He has his manager's support in the endeavour and Marcello Lippi has more or less guaranteed his veteran captain a place in the Italian squad.

Cannavaro has been there and done it with honours including winners' medals for the 2006 World Cup, the 1999 UEFA Cup, 1999 Italian Cup and the Spanish La Liga in 2007 and 2008. In 2006 he was voted European and World Footballer of the Year and Italian Serie A Footballer of the Year.

Cannavaro's career highlight came on his 100th international game when he lifted the 2006 World Cup, and there can be few defenders who could match his 2006 record of not receiving a yellow or red card during the eleven and a half hours that he played in the tournament.

As Italy's most capped player of all time, all that remains for him now is to bow out of the international arena with two captain's World Cup winners' medals in a row.

A rock-solid defender and inspirational captain, Fabio Cannavaro is also renowned for his laid-back style and smiling love of the game.

© Getty Images, Inc

FACT FILE

NAME Didier Yves Drogba Tébily
POSITION Striker
CAPS 60
GOALS 41
CLUB Chelsea
DATE OF BIRTH 11.03.1978
HEIGHT 189 cm
WEIGHT 91 kg
PREVIOUS CLUBS Le Mans, Guingamp, Marseille
INTERNATIONAL DEBUT 08.09.2002 v South Africa
PREVIOUS WORLD CUPS 2006

Even by the odd standards of international football, Didier Drogba is extraordinary. Having spent his youth travelling between Africa and France, he was 21 before signing his first professional contract and settling into the rigorous training needed to make it to the top. He is now national captain and Côte d'Ivoire's all-time leading scorer as well as a United Nations goodwill ambassador.

He's a Chelsea icon who has repaid the £24 million they invested in him in 2004 with a record number of goals for a foreign player. Nobody could deny Drogba's role in reestablishing Chelsea as one of the top four English clubs.

As the Côte d'Ivoire star, captain and assistant coach, Drogba must talk of collective virtues. 'We must be more efficient in possession,' he says. 'Football's not an individual sport you win and lose as a team.' One of the intriguing questions for this World Cup is whether Drogba has it in him to make his team, and by extension Africa as well, into a big footballing force.

Drogba in typically athletic action in a World Cup Qualifier against Malawi.

FACT FILE

NAME Ricardo Alberto Silveira Carvalho
POSITION Defender
CAPS 60
GOALS 4
CLUB Chelsea
DATE OF BIRTH 18.05.1978
HEIGHT 181 cm
WEIGHT 79 kg
PREVIOUS CLUBS, Porto, Leça,
Vitória de Setúbal, Alverca
INTERNATIONAL DEBUT 11.10.2003 v Albania
PREVIOUS WORLD CUPS 2006

© Getty Images, Inc.

Ricardo Carvalho won his first national title at Porto, scooping up four consecutive league titles in the years to 2006, and played in all the games that culminated in an unfancied Portuguese side reaching the European Championship Final in 2004. He finished 2004 being voted best defender at the European Football Awards.

In 2006, Carvalho was even more influential in Portugal's defence as his team steamrollered their way to the 2006 World Cup Semi-finals, the foul on Carvalho saw Wayne Rooney sent off in the controversial 2006 Quarter-final. Carvalho's reputation as the consummate defender will be on the line when he appears for Portugal in South Africa as surely the last chance to prove himself a winner at the highest level of the game.

FACT FILE

FULL NAME Michael Kojo Essien
POSITION Midfielder
CAPS 45
GOALS 8
TEAM Chelsea
DATE OF BIRTH 03.12.1982
HEIGHT 178 cm
WEIGHT 84 kg
PREVIOUS CLUBS Bastia, Lyon
INTERNATIONAL DEBUT 21.01.2002 v Morocco
PREVIOUS WORLD CUPS 2006

© Getty Images, Inc.

Essien's power and aggression have earned him the nickname of 'The Bison'. He's the main midfielder who occupies the centre of the park and is given more encouragement to advance into scoring positions. This nets him a goal on average every four games, typical of which was the long-range drive to secure Ghana's World Cup qualification in the 2–0 win against Sudan in September 2009. By the 2006 World Cup in Germany he was central to Ghana's progress to the second round – he approaches South Africa 2010 in his prime.

SAMUEL ETO'O

SPAIN

© Getty Images, Inc.

FACT FILE
FULL NAME Samuel Eto'o Fils
POSITION Striker
CAPS 87
GOALS 42
CLUB Inter Milan
DATE OF BIRTH 10.03.1981
HEIGHT 180 cm
WEIGHT 75 kg
PREVIOUS CLUBS Real Madrid, Leganés, Espanyol, RCD Mallorca, Barcelona
INTERNATIONAL DEBUT 09.03.1997 v Costa Rica
PREVIOUS WORLD CUPS 1998, 2002

Ten goals in qualification and a newly assumed national captaincy have cemented an impressive national reputation. At 17 years and three months, Eto'o became the youngest player to appear in a World Cup Finals and is the leading scorer in the history of the African Nations Cup, with 16 goals.

At club level Eto'o scored over 100 goals in five seasons with Barcelona, before moving to Inter Milan in 2009. In Italy, the goals kept flowing with a goal-every-other-game career average making him one to watch in South Africa.

© Getty Images, Inc.

FACT FILE
NAME Francesc Fàbregas i Soler
POSITION Midfielder
CAPS 47
GOALS 5
CLUB Arsenal
DATE OF BIRTH 04.05.1987
HEIGHT 177 cm
WEIGHT 69 kg
PREVIOUS CLUBS None
INTERNATIONAL DEBUT 01.03.2006 v Côte d'Ivoire
PREVIOUS WORLD CUPS 2006

Having signed as a schoolboy for Barcelona, Fàbregas left Spain in 2003 aged 16. Andrés Iniesta had already established himself as Barcelona's creative force and Fàbregas was attracted by Arsène Wenger's approach at Arsenal. At international level, however, Iniesta's consistent form has overshadowed Fàbregas. But Fàbregas could yet exceed the master.

He was just 19 years old when he became the youngest Spaniard to play in a World Cup, and two years later at Euro 2008 Fàbregas scored the winning penalty in the Quarter-final shoot-out against Italy. He made the starting eleven in the Final and put in a performance that earned Spain their first major title since 1964.

CESC FÀBREGAS

FACT FILE

NAME Diego Martín Forlán Corazo
POSITION Striker
CAPS 60
GOALS 22
CLUB Atlético Madrid
DATE OF BIRTH 19.05.1979
HEIGHT 179 cm
WEIGHT 75 kg
PREVIOUS CLUBS Independiente, Manchester United, Villarreal
INTERNATIONAL DEBUT 09.03.2002 v Saudi Arabia
PREVIOUS WORLD CUPS 2002

Anyone who writes off Diego Forlán as a Manchester United reject haven't been keeping an eye on Spain's La Liga, where he was top scorer in 2005 with Villarreal and in 2009 with Atlético Madrid. Neither have they paid attention to the South American Qualifiers where he scored a hat-trick against Peru.

At Manchester United he built to a scoring vein of 17 goals in 95 appearances, but when Wayne Rooney arrived at United, Forlán left for Spain, twice winning the European Golden Shoe: in 2004–05 (jointly with Thierry Henry) at Villarreal and in 2008–09 at Atlético Madrid. His image in Spain and Uruguay is of a goal-every-other-game phenomenon and knowledgeable Uruguayan fans tap the space between their eyebrows and say their man has got it 'entre ceja y ceja' to show he has goal-scoring at the front of his mind.

Diego Forlán was born with a sporting spoon in his mouth. His father Pablo played right-back for Uruguay in the 1966 and 1974 World Cups and his grandfather Juan Carlos Corazo played for Independiente in Argentina. Uruguay hopes Forlán has enough 'entre ceja y ceja' to revive a national World Cup tradition.

Diego Forlán's eye for goals means he always keeps his eye on the ball.

FRANCE

FACT FILE

NAME William Éric Gallas
POSITION Defender
CAPS 78
GOALS 4
CLUB Arsenal
DATE OF BIRTH 17.08.1977
HEIGHT 185 cm
WEIGHT 72 kg
PREVIOUS CLUBS Caen, Marseille, Chelsea
INTERNATIONAL DEBUT
12.10.2002 v Slovenia
PREVIOUS WORLD CUPS 2006

© Getty Images, Inc.

Gallas's versatility shows in the way he has operated at right-back, left-back and centre-back for Chelsea; at right-back and centre-back for Arsenal; and at centre-back for France.

Raymond Domenech first paired Gallas with Lilian Thuram in a central partnership that took France through to the 2006 World Cup Final in Germany. The current international partnership is with Éric Abidal and saw a disappointing 10 goals against France in 12 qualifying matches. Now a veteran player, at the age of 32, South Africa will be the last time Gallas represents his country at the highest level.

FACT FILE

NAME Patrice Latyr Evra
POSITION Defender
CAPS 22
GOALS 0
CLUB Manchester United
DATE OF BIRTH 15.05.1981
HEIGHT 173 cm
WEIGHT 76 kg
PREVIOUS CLUBS Marsala,
Monza, Nice, AS Monaco
INTERNATIONAL DEBUT 18 .08.2004
v Bosnia-Herzegovina
PREVIOUS WORLD CUPS None

© Getty Images, Inc.

Patrice Evra was almost not a French player. He was born in Senegal and arrived in Paris aged six when his diplomat father was posted to France. A cosmopolitan career has taken in Marsala in Italy, three French clubs and, from 2006, Manchester United. His game matured as he adapted to English pace, and soon became a club favourite, earning a winner's medal in the 2007, 2008 and 2009 Premier Leagues and the 2008 Champions League with a neat efficiency to his defensive style.

PATRICE EVRA

FACT FILE

NAME Gennaro Ivan Grozni Gattuso
POSITION Midfielder
CAPS 70
GOALS 1
CLUB AC Milan
DATE OF BIRTH 09.01.1978
HEIGHT 177 cm
WEIGHT 77 kg
PREVIOUS CLUBS Perugia, Glasgow Rangers, Salernitana
INTERNATIONAL DEBUT 23.02.2000 v Sweden
PREVIOUS WORLD CUPS 2002, 2006

With a reputation as the hard face of Italian football, it might seem easy to dismiss Gattuso, but there's brain as well as brawn to his game.

Above all, he's a team man who has developed into a fine judge of when to move forward in support of his strikers and when to remain in defence. Early on in his career, at the age of 19, Gattuso proved he was his own man when he quit Perugia to join Glasgow Rangers. A run of 40 Scottish Premier League games helped mould his robust style.

Gattuso returned to Italy with Salernitana in 1998. Though the newly promoted team was relegated after a season, he caught AC Milan's eye and signed for them in 1999. Then manager Carlo Ancelotti (now of Chelsea) used him as a ball-winning foil to Andrea Pirlo and in the process formed a decade-long partnership for club and country.

Gattuso is a battler at the deep end of football and a huge favourite with Italian fans who respond to the passion he brings to his terminator role. They're still talking about his exhibitionism after Italy lifted the World Cup in 2006, when, in a show of mad exuberance, he ripped his shorts off and danced ecstatically around the pitch.

Gattuso's nickname 'Ringhio' means 'snarler' in Italian, but he's a fan favourite and sure to be one to watch in South Africa.

KAKÁ

BRAZIL

© Getty Images, Inc.

FACT FILE

NAME Ricardo Izecson Santos Leite (Kaká)

POSITION Midfielder

CAPS 75

GOALS 26

CLUB Real Madrid

DATE OF BIRTH 22 .04.1982

HEIGHT 186 cm

WEIGHT 83 kg

PREVIOUS CLUBS São Paulo, AC Milan

INTERNATIONAL DEBUT 31.01.2002 v Bolivia

PREVIOUS WORLD CUPS 2002, 2006

Kaká is a singular man. He's not the stereotypical Brazilian star who kicked and charmed his way up from the slums, but a middle-class boy who spent some of his first wealth on his brother's college education.

He signed to São Paolo aged 15, and made his senior debut in January 2001

In recognition of Kaká's fame, ability and work for the United Nations' World Food Programme, Time magazine places Kaká on a list of the world's 100 most influential people.

Every game guarantees defence-splitting passes and he scores consistently from distance, with a one-in-three-games strike rate to underline just how attack-minded a midfielder he really is. He moved to AC Milan in 2003 and, as the focal point of attack switching between the midfield and striker roles, he helped them to Serie A and Champions League titles. He seemed set to remain in Italy, but in June 2009 Real Madrid paid a reported £56 million for its latest superstar.

Kaká travelled to South Africa for the 2009 Confederations Cup, where he shone, and was named the Player of the Tournament, plus Man of the Match in the Final after helping Brazil to a 3–2 win against the United States.

Kaká shone in the 2009 Confederations Cup in South Africa and was named Player of the Tournament.

FACT FILE

NAME Thierry Daniel Henry
POSITION Striker
CAPS 117
GOALS 51
CLUB Barcelona
DATE OF BIRTH 17.08.1977
HEIGHT 188 cm
WEIGHT 83 kg
PREVIOUS CLUBS Monaco, Juventus, Arsenal
INTERNATIONAL DEBUT
11.10.1997 v South Africa
PREVIOUS WORLD CUPS 1998, 2002, 2006

© Getty Images, Inc.

Starting as a winger, Henry made his debut for France as a 20 year old and was top scorer, with three goals in each tournament, when France triumphed in the 1998 World Cup and Euro 2000. Any doubts over his ability to play under pressure were resolved in the 2006 World Cup when he scored three goals, including the winner, against Brazil, the defending champions.

As France fell into relative international decline, Henry retained enough stellar presence for Raymond Domenech to promote him to national captain, and he will be looking to redeem his reputation both as a player and a man of honour in South Africa.

FACT FILE

NAME Andrés Iniesta Lujan
POSITION Midfielder
CAPS 39
GOALS 6
CLUB Barcelona
DATE OF BIRTH 11.05.1984
HEIGHT 170 cm
WEIGHT 65 kg
PREVIOUS CLUBS None
INTERNATIONAL DEBUT 27.05.2006 v Russia
PREVIOUS WORLD CUPS 2006

© Getty Images, Inc.

One of the game's great all-rounders with skills underpinned by consistency and loyalty. Andrés Iniesta has proved himself a big-game player who does not freeze when the spotlight is brightest. He was on form during the early World Cup Qualifiers but a thigh injury restricted him in the later games and he missed the Confederations Cup.

He's also been there and done it for his club in two Champions League Finals (2006, 2009) and for his country at the European Championship (2008). Spain hopes that he can do it again and that in South Africa he will once more show his talents to the world.

GERMANY

FACT FILE
NAME Miroslav Marian Klose
POSITION Striker
CAPS 93
GOALS 48
CLUB Bayern Munich
DATE OF BIRTH 09.06.1978
HEIGHT 182 cm
WEIGHT 74 kg
PREVIOUS CLUBS Werder Bremen, 1. FC Kaiserslautern, FC Homburg
INTERNATIONAL DEBUT 24.03.2001 v Albania
PREVIOUS WORLD CUPS 2002, 2006

© Getty Images, Inc.

Miroslav Klose's World Cup goal-getting is impressive and he's the only player to have scored five in consecutive tournaments. If he repeats the feat a third time, he'll be in reach of Ronaldo's record tally of 16 World Cup goals.

In the 2008 European tournament, Klose played in an emotional game against Poland, his country of birth, but proved his loyalties were not divided with two passes that put Lukas Podolski through for both German goals. Fans point out that despite being left-footed, three of the five goals Klose scored at the last World Cup came from his right foot, hinting that there's plenty more to come.

FACT FILE
NAME Dirk Kuyt
POSITION Striker
CAPS 59
GOALS 13
CLUB Liverpool
DATE OF BIRTH 22.07.1980
HEIGHT 184 cm
WEIGHT 77 kg
PREVIOUS CLUBS Utrecht, Feyenoord
INTERNATIONAL DEBUT 03.09.2004 v Liechtenstein
PREVIOUS WORLD CUPS 2006

© Getty Images, Inc.

He netted three goals in the 2010 World Cup Qualifiers and, in a drawn summer 2009 friendly against England, snapped up a Rio Ferdinand back pass to bag another. England be warned. Yet for all his frenetic activity, Kuyt has a cool head and is a penalty specialist calm enough to have scored from two spot kicks in a 2–1 Merseyside derby.

The Dutch have a long tradition of failure at penalty shoot-outs and at Euro 2000 missed a total of five penalties in the final against Italy. If Kuyt can help save Holland from another such fiasco in South Africa, he will seal his status as national legend.

DIRK KUYT

© Getty Images, Inc.

FACT FILE

NAME Philipp Lahm
POSITION Defender
CAPS 63
GOALS 3
CLUB Bayern Munich
DATE OF BIRTH 11.11.1983
HEIGHT 170 cm
WEIGHT 61 kg
PREVIOUS CLUB VfB Stuttgart
INTERNATIONAL DEBUT 18.02.2004 v Croatia
PREVIOUS WORLD CUPS 2006

Lahm signed on for Bayern Munich when he was 11 years old, playing in the junior sides as a defensive midfielder, right midfielder or right full-back. On moving to VfB Stuttgart for a couple of years, he was deployed as the left-back, and he remained in this position when he returned to Bayern in 2005. That is where he has gained his reputation for being one of the best full-backs in the world, a fact recognised by his nomination for the UEFA Team of the Year in the seasons he has been fit (2004, 2006, 2007 and 2008), putting him alongside Michael Ballack as most nominated German player.

He was named Left-back of the Year in 2008 in recognition of his play during Euro 2008. He clinched the Semi-final against Turkey with a last-gasp goal: with the game at 2–2, Lahm played a high-speed one-two with Thomas Hitzlsperger to take the ball into the penalty area and fire past the Turkish 'keeper at the near post. It gave him the confidence to go forward in the Final against Spain, though he was at fault when a communication breakdown with his 'keeper Jens Lehmann allowed Fernando Torres to get behind him and chip in the game's only goal.

That goal denied Lahm the international winner's medal he wants to put alongside three Bundesliga medals, his World Cup third-place medal from 2006 and his second-place medal at Euro 2008.

Lahm's last-minute goal took Germany to the Euro 2008 Final against Spain in Vienna.

FACT FILE

NAME Lionel Andrés Messi
POSITION Midfielder
CAPS 43
GOALS 13
CLUB Barcelona
DATE OF BIRTH 24.06.1987
HEIGHT 169 cm
WEIGHT 67 kg
PREVIOUS CLUBS None
INTERNATIONAL DEBUT
17.08.2005 v Hungary
PREVIOUS WORLD CUPS 2006

© Getty Images, Inc.

Messi's amazing balance sees him able to skip past challenges and power through to fire shots at goal.

Lionel Messi's skills on the ball are astonishing. He's one of the most exciting players of his generation and his quality is apparent from the farthest corners of the largest stadiums.

Introduced to Barcelona in 2000, the 12-year-old began his training proper. In 2004 he became the youngest player to appear in a La Liga match, and the youngest to score a league goal. That season Barcelona won La Liga, then the Champions League the following season. Messi has gone from strength to strength and is key to Barcelona's dominance in Europe.

International progress was less assured: he came on as a substitute against Hungary in 2005 only to be sent off two minutes later for elbowing a defender. He played a minor part in Argentina's 2006 World Cup campaign, but four years on he is fully established in the national side, the only Argentinian to play in all 18 qualifying matches. Maradona gave him the number 10 shirt for the World Cup Qualifier against Venezuela and Messi repaid the favour by opening the scoring in a 4–0 win.

Messi's power, balance and strength soon drew comparisons between him and Maradona. 'Messidona' is the clumsy nickname to catch the elegance of the ball-playing prodigy who, in a 2007 Spanish Cup Semi-final against Getafe, scored a goal to compare with Maradona's 'Goal of the Century' against England in the 1986 World Cup. Both players ran over 60 metres to dribble past opponents before shooting from similar position on the right to score and then wheel off towards the corner flag.

There will more than likely be goals from Messi in South Africa – something astonishing to witness and remember from a player with talent enough to fit the Argentine number 10 shirt.

FACT FILE

NAME Lucimar Ferreira da Silva (Lùcio)
POSITION Defender
CAPS 88
GOALS 4
CLUB Inter Milan
DATE OF BIRTH 08.05.1978
HEIGHT 188 cm
WEIGHT 81 kg
PREVIOUS CLUBS Internacional (Brazil),
Bayer Leverkusen, Bayern Munich
INTERNATIONAL DEBUT 15.11.2002 v Colombia
PREVIOUS WORLD CUPS 2002, 2006

© Getty Images, Inc.

England fans might remember Lúcio for a mistake that allowed Michael Owen to score the opening goal in the 2002 World Cup Quarter-final. Brazilian fans recall an otherwise flawless campaign highlighted with an heroic stand in the Final against Germany when he took the full impact of a free kick and yet stayed on meaning he played for all 630 minutes of the tournament.

His centre-half's skills have been influenced by 10 years in European football. At Bayern Munich he won three Bundesliga titles and three German Cups. A move to the Italian club Inter Milan in summer 2009 can only have further refined the skills, as Lúcio, now in the autumn of a distinguished career, approaches a third World Cup – his first as captain.

FACT FILE

NAME John Michael Nchekwube Obinna (Mikel)
POSITION Midfielder
CAPS 28
GOALS 2
CLUB Chelsea
DATE OF BIRTH 22.04.1987
HEIGHT 188 cm
WEIGHT 86 kg
PREVIOUS CLUB Lyn Oslo
INTERNATIONAL DEBUT 17 August 2005 v Libya
PREVIOUS WORLD CUPS None

© Getty Images, Inc.

At the 2003 Under-17 FIFA World Championship in Finland, the Nigerian FA misspelled one of his given names as Mikel. When he moved to Chelsea in 2006, he had become Mikel John Obi or John Obi Mikel, finally settling on Mikel.

Mikel's qualities have long been apparent and the public scrap for the 18-year-old's signature between Chelsea and Manchester United showed how highly he was regarded – as did the £16 million Chelsea paid when they eventually got their man. Nigerians are certainly hoping Mikel is up to his biggest test yet.

ARGENTINA

© Getty Images, Inc

FACT FILE

NAME Javier Alejandro Mascherano
POSITION Midfielder
CAPS 55
GOALS 2
CLUB Liverpool
DATE OF BIRTH 08.06.1984
HEIGHT 171 cm
WEIGHT 66 kg
PREVIOUS CLUBS West Ham United, Corinthians, River Plate
INTERNATIONAL DEBUT 16.07.2003 v Uruguay
PREVIOUS WORLD CUPS 2006

Diego Maradona's first managerial move towards the end of 2008 was to appoint Javier Mascherano as team captain.

Only Messi was on the field for longer than Mascherano during Argentina's rocky World Cup qualifying campaign. Though he stuttered in the early games, he regained form for the 2–1 victory over Peru and in the 1–0 win in Uruguay – more than enough to vindicate his manager's faith and to secure his claim to the captain's armband in South Africa.

FACT FILE

NAME Andrea Pirlo
POSITION Midfielder
CAPS 64
GOALS 8
CLUB AC Milan
DATE OF BIRTH 19.05.1979
HEIGHT 177 cm
WEIGHT 68 kg
PREVIOUS CLUBS Brescia, Inter Milan, Reggina
INTERNATIONAL DEBUT
07.09.2002 v Azerbaijan
PREVIOUS WORLD CUPS 2006

© Getty Images, Inc

Andrea Pirlo provides game-winning inspiration and epitomises a style so successful that it earned Italy the last World Cup. As a club then international defensive midfielder, he delivered defensive support with his powerful running and trustworthy tackling.

In qualifying games for 2010, Pirlo has been pushed forward to his old position as a playmaker behind the strikers. This allows him less time on the ball but gives him greater scope to set up goal-scoring opportunities in the contested ground immediately ahead of him. And that's where we're likely to see Pirlo when he lines up for Italy in South Africa.

ITALY

ANDREA PIRLO

© Getty Images, Inc.

FACT FILE

NAME Steven Pienaar
POSITION Midfielder
CAPS 46
GOALS 2
CLUB Everton
DATE OF BIRTH 17.03.1982
HEIGHT 176 cm
WEIGHT 66 kg
PREVIOUS CLUBS
Borussia Dortmund, Ajax
INTERNATIONAL DEBUT 23.05.2002 v Turkey
PREVIOUS WORLD CUPS
2002

Steven Pienaar is a midfield regular in a South African team that has its greatest strength in midfielders. He's a senior member of the South African squad, with the European experience lacking in many of his younger team-mates. His reputation as a boy wonder at Ajax Cape Town, a feeder club for Ajax Amsterdam, put him on the European conveyor belt. He was part of an attack-minded Ajax team that won the Dutch League in 2002 and 2004 and reached the Quarter-finals of the 2003 Champions League. Then he spent a frustrating year at Borussia Dortmund before moving to Everton in 2007.

His quick passing game has established him as a fixture in a creative Everton midfield and when he advances forward the Toffees' fans anticipate one of his fierce shots on goal. His gathering confidence at club level has helped his country, and he played a key role in the 2009 Confederations Cup and the 2010 African Cup of Nations.

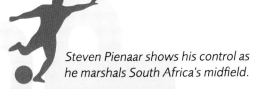

Steven Pienaar shows his control as he marshals South Africa's midfield.

FRANCK RIBÉRY

© Getty Images, Inc.

FACT FILE

NAME Franck Bilal Ribéry
POSITION Midfielder
CAPS 41
GOALS 7
CLUB Bayern Munich
DATE OF BIRTH 07.04.1983
HEIGHT 170 cm
WEIGHT 72 kg
PREVIOUS CLUBS
Boulogne-sur-Mer, Alès, Stade Brestois,
Metz, Galatasaray, Marseille
INTERNATIONAL DEBUT
27.05.2006 v Mexico
PREVIOUS WORLD CUPS 2006

Contractual problems had Ribéry bouncing between clubs until he made his name during two years with Marseilles between 2005 and 2007. He then settled at Bayern and in his first season won the German double, was voted Bundesliga Player of the Year, and became only the second foreign player to be named German Footballer of the Year, claiming the prize ahead of Michael Ballack.

Although his international debut was less than a month before the 2006 World Cup, such was his impact that he earned selection in the team that lost so narrowly to Italy in the Finals. His first international goal was in the knockout round when he outwitted the Spanish 'keeper Iker Casillas to pull France level and set up a 3–1 victory. Then came the Semi-final against Brazil when he asserted himself like a seasoned professional. Soon all France knew about Ribéry, who emerged from the tournament with a ringing endorsement from legendary Zinédine Zidane.

For most people, the expectation that accompanies that kind of recognition might be too heavy a weight – Ribéry is different. Despite scoring in the early 2010 Qualifiers, injury has kept him out of the last few games and France looks forward to his return in South Africa.

A compact midfielder who combines speed of thought with speed of action, Ribéry is a valuable playmaker.

FACT FILE

NAME Lukas Podolski
POSITION Striker
CAPS 69
GOALS 37
CLUB Köln
DATE OF BIRTH 04.06.1985
HEIGHT 182 cm
WEIGHT 82 kg
PREVIOUS CLUB Bayern Munich
INTERNATIONAL DEBUT 06.06.2004 v Hungary
PREVIOUS WORLD CUPS 2006

© Getty Images, Inc.

Lukas Podolski is a creative striker whose partnership with Miroslav Klose could hold the key to Germany's progress in South Africa. He signed for Köln aged 10, and at 18 made Bundesliga history when he scored 10 goals in his first 19 games. In the 2006 World Cup he partnered Miroslav Klose in attack, scoring a goal against Ecuador and both goals in the 2–0 Quarter-final win over Sweden, and was named the World Cup's Best Young Player.

He performed well during the 2010 Qualifiers, scoring the first two goals in Germany's game against Liechtenstein, and the opener in the 2–1 home win over Russia.

FACT FILE

NAME Arjen Robben
POSITION Striker
CAPS 45
GOALS 11
CLUB Bayern Munich
DATE OF BIRTH 23.01.1984
HEIGHT 180 cm
WEIGHT 75 kg
PREVIOUS CLUBS Groningen, PSV Eindhoven, Chelsea, Real Madrid
INTERNATIONAL DEBUT 06.09.2003 v Austria
PREVIOUS WORLD CUPS 2006

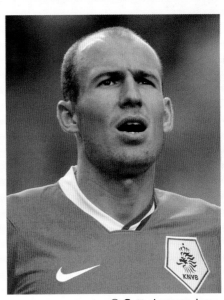

© Getty Images, Inc.

At the 2006 World Cup against Serbia and Montenegro, Robben scored the winning goal and was Man of the Match. He received the award a second time against Côte d'Ivoire, to become one of only eight players in the tournament to have won the Man of the Match award more than once.

At Euro 2008 Robben had to battle Robin van Persie for his place on the left. Both are versatile players and Bert van Marwijk accommodated both in the last two World Cup qualifying games against Scotland and Norway making it likely that both will be in the starting line-ups in South Africa.

DENMARK

FACT FILE

NAME Christian Bager Poulsen
POSITION Defender
CAPS 71
GOALS 5
CLUB Juventus
DATE OF BIRTH 28.02.1980
HEIGHT 182 cm
WEIGHT 76 kg
PREVIOUS CLUBS Copenhagen, FC Schalke 04, Sevilla
INTERNATIONAL DEBUT 10.11.2001 v Netherlands
PREVIOUS WORLD CUPS 2002

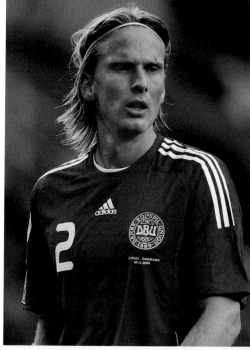

© Getty Images, Inc.

Christian Poulsen is a national favourite, and his presence is Denmark's greatest hope in South Africa. A patchy discipline record and aggressive streak has led to crowd trouble, match forfeits and suspensions, nonetheless, Poulsen has remained an automatic and popular choice for his country. Denmark's tactics revolve around his charismatic presence and his two-footed passing ability made him key to an early World Cup qualification from a strong group that included Portugal and Sweden.

FACT FILE

NAME Robson de Souza (Robinho)
POSITION Striker
CAPS 72
GOALS 19
CLUB Manchester City
DATE OF BIRTH 25.01.1984
HEIGHT 173 cm
WEIGHT 60 kg
PREVIOUS CLUBS Santos, Real Madrid
INTERNATIONAL DEBUT 13.07.2003 v Mexico
PREVIOUS WORLD CUPS 2006

© Getty Images, Inc.

Robinho is an attacker whom defensive players fear and he enters this World Cup with the impressive track record of leading Santos to their first Brazilian title since Pelé played for the club, plus two titles with Real Madrid. Internationally, he has won the Copa América and two Confederations Cups. So there's definitely a space to fill in the trophy cabinet.

Despite club success, his heart really belongs to Brazil and he wants to improve on the last World Cup, when he was a substitute for the majority of the games and did not score. Since then he has been national captain for a friendly and played in every game of the 2009 Confederations Cup in South Africa. His biggest test now looms.

ROBINHO

RONALDO

FACT FILE

NAME Cristiano Ronaldo dos Santos Aveiro
POSITION Striker
CAPS 68
GOALS 22
CLUB Real Madrid
DATE OF BIRTH 05.02.1985
HEIGHT 184 cm
WEIGHT 78 kg
PREVIOUS CLUBS Sporting CP, Manchester United
INTERNATIONAL DEBUT 16.08.2003 v Kazakhstan
PREVIOUS WORLD CUPS 2006

© Getty Images, Inc.

A claim that Ronaldo is the world's best footballer can't rely on statistically based evidence alone. But it's a good start. At Manchester United, Ronaldo scored 118 times in 291 appearances and his 84 Premier League goals helped his club to three consecutive titles from 2007. In 2008, Ronaldo was the FIFA World Player of the Year and moved to Real Madrid in summer 2009 for a world record fee of £80 million.

He has a huge bag of tricks at his command – his trademark stepovers and distinctive 'twinkle toes' running style serve to emphasise his pace and ability to confuse defenders. Equally comfortable on either foot and a good header too, he is difficult to defend against.

Ronaldo says: 'I don't play football just because I like it. I play because I've got an ambition to always win and be the best and to win every trophy and competition I'm part of. I'll be happy when I win the Champions League, the European Championship and the World Cup.'

Ronaldo's unique style and sublime skills will test all opposing teams. His quick thinking can turn a game on its head in an instant.

© Getty Images, Inc.

FACT FILE

NAME Carlos Alberto Tévez
POSITION Striker
CAPS 51
GOALS 8
CLUB Manchester City
DATE OF BIRTH 05.02.1984
HEIGHT 173 cm
WEIGHT 74 kg
PREVIOUS CLUBS
Manchester United, West Ham United, Corinthians, Boca Juniors
INTERNATIONAL DEBUT
06.06.2004 v Paraguay
PREVIOUS WORLD CUPS
2006

Carlos Tévez's whirlwind British career has seen him inspire West Ham United to Premiership survival in 2007 and score the only goal in a last-game-of-the-season clincher against Manchester United. He is still revered in East London and was West Ham's Hammer of the Year in 2007. He then moved north and helped Manchester United to two Premiership titles and the Champions League, before switching to Manchester City in summer 2009. Tévez is a hero in South America too, named the Brazilian Football Confederation league's best player, the first non-Brazilian to win the award since 1976.

His competitive streak saw him sent off twice in a three-game stretch during 2010 World Cup qualifying, first against Colombia in November 2007 after he kicked the full-back and a year later for a rash tackle in a 1–1 draw with Paraguay. Thereafter, Maradona tended to use him as a substitute. Perhaps this is where he'll remain, although it seems unlikely that a talent such as Tévez will spend too much time on the bench in South Africa.

Tévez is a powerful striker who attacks full tilt and with explosive skill.

FACT FILE

FULL NAME Roque Luis Santa Cruz Cantero
POSITION Striker
CAPS 66
GOALS 20
CLUB Manchester City
DATE OF BIRTH 16.08.1981
HEIGHT 189 cm
WEIGHT 80 kg
PREVIOUS CLUBS Olimpia Asunción, Bayern Munich, Blackburn Rovers
INTERNATIONAL DEBUT 04.1999 v Mexico
PREVIOUS WORLD CUPS 2002, 2006

© Getty Images, Inc.

Roque Santa Cruz scored three goals for the national side on his debut in the Copa América at the age of 17 in 1999, and later that year won the Paraguayan Footballer of the Year award. He spent eight years at Bayern Munich, helping his team win the German league and cup double, the UEFA Champions League and the Intercontinental Cup.

He played in both the 2002 and 2006 World Cup Finals, scored a hat-trick against Colombia in a 5–0 victory during the Copa América 2007, and was one of Paraguay's top scorers in the 2010 World Cup Qualifiers.

FACT FILE

NAME Wesley Sneijder
POSITION Midfielder
CAPS 56
GOALS 12
CLUB Inter Milan
DATE OF BIRTH 09.06.1984
WEIGHT 67 kg
PREVIOUS CLUBS Ajax, Real Madrid
INTERNATIONAL DEBUT
30.04.2003 v Portugal
PREVIOUS WORLD CUPS 2006

© Getty Images, Inc.

Wesley Sneijder made his Netherlands debut before his 19th birthday and within a year was scoring goals in the Euro 2004 qualifying matches. He appeared twice as substitute in the Netherlands' final run to the 2004 Semi-finals and started all four games at the 2006 World Cup in Germany. At Euro 2008, Sneijder marked his 24th birthday with a remarkable goal in the 3–0 rout of Italy. For fans following their fancied side through their South Africa 2010 adventure, only more of Sneijder's best will be good enough.

ROQUE SANTA CRUZ

NETHERLANDS

WESLEY SNEIJDER

NETHERLANDS

FACT FILE

NAME Robin van Persie
POSITION Midfielder
CAPS 41
GOALS 14
CLUB Arsenal
DATE OF BIRTH 06.08.1983
HEIGHT 183 cm
WEIGHT 71 kg
PREVIOUS CLUB Feyenoord
INTERNATIONAL DEBUT 04.06.2005 v Romania
PREVIOUS WORLD CUPS 2006

© Getty Images, Inc.

Despite injuries, the move to Arsenal has been a success. Robin van Persie was voted Arsenal's Player of the Season in 2009, and really proved himself in January 2009 when he either scored or assisted every Arsenal goal that month.

His goal-scoring header during a qualifying match against Scotland had Dutch fans wondering whether van Persie should be taking corners or receiving them. South Africa 2010 should answer the question of whether van Persie will go down in Dutch football history as a goal provider or goal grabber.

FACT FILE

NAME Bastian Schweinsteiger
POSITION Midfielder
CAPS 73
GOALS 19
CLUB Bayern Munich
DATE OF BIRTH 01.08.1984
HEIGHT 183 cm
WEIGHT 79 kg
PREVIOUS CLUBS None
INTERNATIONAL DEBUT 06.06.2004 v Hungary
PREVIOUS WORLD CUPS 2006

© Getty Images, Inc.

Bastian Schweinsteiger took Euro 2004 by storm, setting up the opening goal for his Bayern colleague Michael Ballack. Schweinsteiger scored his first two international goals against Russia to start a surprising run in which Germany have not lost a game when he has scored.

After being sent off in Germany's Euro 2008 group match against Croatia, he returned from suspension to score the first goal in a 3–2 Quarter-final victory over Portugal, and also scored the first goal in the 3–2 Semi-final victory against Turkey.

BASTIAN SCHWEINSTEIGER

FACT FILE

NAME Fernando José Torres Sanz
POSITION Striker
CAPS 71
GOALS 23
CLUB Liverpool
DATE OF BIRTH 20.03.1984
HEIGHT 185 cm
WEIGHT 78 kg
PREVIOUS CLUB Atlético Madrid
INTERNATIONAL DEBUT
06.09.2003 v Portugal
PREVIOUS WORLD CUPS 2006

Fernando Torres is synonymous with goals, including the single goal that secured his country the Euro 2008 Final.

As a schoolboy, Torres was a goalkeeper before converting to striker. He scored 75 goals in 174 La Liga appearances for Atlético Madrid and joined Liverpool in 2007. In his debut season, he became Liverpool's first player since Robbie Fowler to score more than 20 league goals in a season. His 29 goals for the 2007–08 season took him past Michael Owen's record.

Torres made his debut for Spain against Portugal in 2003 and the 2010 World Cup will be his fourth major tournament so he'll be using the experiences gleaned at Euro 2004, the 2006 World Cup and Euro 2008. At 26 years of age, when he pulls on his number nine shirt in South Africa, he will be one of his country's most experienced players.

At club level, he is a hero in a Liverpool side where he plays number nine to Steven Gerrard's number eight. In June 2009, Torres said he and good friend Gerrard had already been bantering about a Spain v England Final.

Torres scored a hat-trick to help Spain extend their unbeaten run to 33 matches after defeating New Zealand 5–0 in their Confederations Cup opener.

DAVID VILLA

© Getty Images, Inc.

FACT FILE

NAME David Villa Sànchez
POSITION Striker
CAPS 54
GOALS 35
CLUB Valencia
DATE OF BIRTH 03.12.1981
HEIGHT 175 cm
WEIGHT 69 kg
PREVIOUS CLUBS
Sporting Gijón, Zaragoza
INTERNATIONAL DEBUT
09.02.2005 v San Marino
PREVIOUS WORLD CUPS
2006

Villa's goal-scoring record is putting him up with the game's great names. He has hit over a hundred goals for Valencia, a club he remains loyal to despite persistent interest from bigger sides. For Spain, he has scored an astonishing 33 goals in 52 games. He scored three goals at the 2006 World Cup, and was top scorer at Euro 2008 with four. In February 2009, he scored in a record-breaking sixth successive international game in Spain's 2–0 win against England.

The usual selfishness of a talented natural goal scorer is well hidden, and Villa is famous for avoiding the limelight off the pitch. His personality seems to be an ego-free zone and he prefers talking of 'we' rather than 'I' when describing his partnership with fellow high-scorer, Fernando Torres. A partnership might well provide the goals that earn Spain their first ever World Cup.

Villa swoops back to the centre circle having just scored against South Africa in the 2009 Confederations Cup.

FACT FILE

NAME Xavier Hernández i Creus
POSITION Midfielder
CAPS 83
GOALS 8
CLUB Barcelona
DATE OF BIRTH 25.01.1980
HEIGHT 170 cm
WEIGHT 68 kg
PREVIOUS CLUBS None
INTERNATIONAL DEBUT
15.11.2000 v Netherlands
PREVIOUS WORLD CUPS 2002, 2006

© Getty Images, Inc.

Xavi made his debut for Spain aged 20, having led the junior side to victory at the 1999 FIFA World Youth Championship in Nigeria and a silver medal at the 2000 Olympics. He was Spain's most influential player in the 2006 World Cup, appearing in every game until Spain went out to France in the second round.

His Euro 2008 partnership with Andrés Iniesta brought a string of passes to the attackers – he scored the Semi-final opener against Russia, and in the Final against Germany his pass to Fernando Torres secured Spain the winning goal. His methods of keeping possession and controlling games continued during Spain's flawless World Cup qualification.

FACT FILE

NAME Javier Adelmar Zanetti
POSITION Defender
CAPS 136
GOALS 5
CLUB Inter Milan
DATE OF BIRTH 10.08.1973
HEIGHT 178 cm
WEIGHT 75 kg
PREVIOUS CLUBS Banfield, Talleres RE
INTERNATIONAL DEBUT
16.11.1994 v Chile
PREVIOUS WORLD CUPS 2002, 1998

© Getty Images, Inc.

Zanetti has led Inter to four Serie A titles and has played in over 600 matches, which is more than any other non-Italian born player. He debuted for Argentina in 1994 under the management of Daniel Passarella and was a regular at the 1998 and 2002 World Cups. He played in the qualification rounds for 2006, but was controversially ignored by José Pekerman. A recall came against France in 2007 under Alfio Basile and he provided the assist for Javier Saviola to score the only goal of the game. He was vice-captain for the Copa América 2007, and has remained a regular under Diego Maradona.

XAVI HERNÁNDEZ

ARGENTINA

JAVIER ZANETTI

INDEX